the
Response

PRACTISING
MINDFULNESS
IN YOUR DAILY LIFE

Library and Archives Canada Cataloguing in Publication

Petingola, Gary, 1958-, author
The Response / Gary Petingola.

ISBN 978-1-9889892-2-8(softcover)

I. Title.

LCC BF637.M56 P48 2020   DDC 158.1/3-dc23

Printed and bound in Canada on 100% recycled paper.

Book Design: Kasandra Diane Henry
Cover Design: Heather Campbell and Gary Petingola
Cover and Interior Artwork: Hannah Petingola
Author Photo: Hannah Petingola

Published by:
StoriaBooks
an imprint of Latitude 46 Publishing
info@latitude46publishing.com
Latitude46publishing.com

the
Response

PRACTISING
MINDFULNESS
IN YOUR DAILY LIFE

Gary Petingola

StoriaBooks

For my Wise Wife and our daughters, Blue Eyes and Brown Eyes, their

partners and children!

CONTENTS

CONTENTS

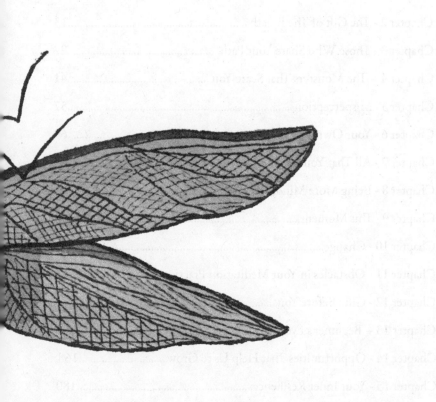

INTRODUCTION

I remember that day as if it were yesterday. I was working as a social worker in a hospital dialysis unit when her email message abruptly arrived. Who would have known how this unexpected interruption to the monotony of my workday would have set in motion such a ripple effect. I didn't know her then, and even as I write these words, today, we have never met. She was living several thousand kilometers away. Yet, in that moment, she made a conscious decision to share her story with all on an international online forum, a list server for professional social workers from across the globe. There was no going back. Her vulnerability unmasked. Walls taken down and her inner person exposed.

She was a middle-aged healthcare worker trying to deal with the everyday struggles of life complicated by recent job loss, financial hardship, the deaths of several family members, and the devastation of a recent hurricane. The text of her email message focused on the unpleasantness of being without employment and feelings of being squeezed out of her profession by bureaucracy. She shared feelings of hopelessness and pessimism about finding future work in her field, disadvantaged by the shadows of ageism. Her message was raw – heartfelt. It was shared for all to see. Like a train grinding to an abrupt halt, all messaging activity simply stopped. The silence was deafening. This forum usually buzzing with professional activity suddenly became uncomfortably silent. I found the silence to be even more distressing than the contents of her message. It puzzled me that a group of individuals dedicated to helping others had seemingly become speechless, frozen, and unresponsive. Time elapsed. I waited curiously for a response. Nothing. For me, it felt like the sky had opened up and the universe had unleashed contents of a violent storm but no one noticed.

Jon Kabat-Zinn defines mindfulness as the awareness that arises through paying attention, on purpose, in the present moment, non-judgmentally. One of the main proponents of mindfulness, he is essentially responsible for its westernization and introduction to mainstream America in the late 1970's. As a molecular biologist at MIT in Boston, he gained an interest in how the application of meditation and yoga practices might be helpful in alleviating suffering. He developed the Mindfulness-Based Stress Reduction (MBSR) eight-week program. Since its inception, this evidence-based curriculum has helped thousands of people all over the world in combating the harmful effects of chronic stress as well as a variety of medical conditions. MBSR can also be beneficial for healthcare workers in targeting emotional exhaustion, psychological distress, depression, anxiety, and occupational stress. My recollection of Jon Kabat-Zinn, having completed a 7-day professional training retreat with him, is one of warmth, passion and openness. His teachings and his wisdom have influenced the way I live my life. Instead of running away from the present, mindfulness practice invited me to be in the moment with radical acceptance and trust. A complete reversal of how I had been living my life up until that point. My incline was to run both metaphorically and literally from the unpleasantness of life. This contributed to my suffering.

Seeing that email, and the subsequent silence that followed, I used what I had learned from mindfulness and focused on the present. A turning inward – an invitation to drop into what I was experiencing in mind, body, and heart. Mindfulness is often synonymous with "heartfulness" and, in that moment, my heart felt heavy, my body rigid, and my thoughts busy. I felt a sense of deep connection as a mindfulness teacher and social worker to this stranger, thousands of kilometers away. Part of me wanted to ignore this "outing" and carry on with my day, unscathed and comfortable with what I knew. Yet another part of me felt compelled to sit with this discomfort with curiosity and compassion. I was reminded that we all suffer in some capacity. None of us is absolved from this component of our human condition. I paused, went to the breath, observed, and decided to reply to all, carefully crafting a written response and in that moment – all changed. I came to understand that your pain and suffering is my pain and suffering. I was reminded that we are all interconnected. We share a commonality – a kinship – a wholeness. I responded:

Dear Friend I am not sure that our paths have crossed but I certainly feel your anguish. I wish I could offer you a job but I cannot. But what I would like to do is invite all of your colleagues to offer a virtual Loving Kindness meditation for you today at 3:00 p.m. I know this might sound farfetched and it is a bit of a risk on my part but I truly think that the collective power of the group will hopefully comfort you and offer you strength during these challenging times. So, I am setting my watch alarm for 2:55 p.m. EST and I am inviting online members to do the same! Today at 3:00 EST turn off your phones, pagers and close your office doors. Forfeit your coffee breaks and office chatter. Begin by sitting down in a comfortable position, closing your eyes. Take a few deep breaths, to anchor you to the present moment. Repeat to yourself over and over again "May I be safe. May I be happy. May I be healthy.

May my life be filled with ease." If your attention wanders don't worry about it. When you recognize your mind has drifted off, gently escort it back to the breath, see if you can gently let go and begin again. "May I be safe, be happy, be healthy, live with ease." Then call to mind our friend in pain. You can visualize what she looks like, say her name to yourself. Imagine that she is sitting in front of you. Get a feeling for her presence, and then direct the phrases of loving kindness to her. "May you live in safety, be happy, be healthy, live with ease."

By 3:00 p.m. I had made my way to a quiet cocoon known as the Indigenous medicine lodge located in the heart of the busy urban hospital where I worked, away from overhead pagers, busy halls and constant interruptions. I adopted a sitting meditation posture with my body upright and dignified, feet firmly planted, hands resting on thighs, chin tucked slightly, eyes softened, lips parted. In between layers of choiceless awareness, using the breath as an anchor if my mind ruminated, I intentionally sent loving kindness meditation intentions to this friend in need.

I later learned that seventy-one percent of approximately seven hundred healthcare professionals connected on this list server from Canada, the United States, India, the Northern Mariana Islands, Australia and the Netherlands, unplugged during their busy workday to collectively meditate in unison on that early summer afternoon in June 2011. There was the option to not respond to the initial post; however, I responded and this act culminated in the creation of a weekly mindfulness meditation community that has been sustained, evolved, and become a virtual sangha (a group of people who come together to meditate) that continues today, a quantum entanglement that has transcended time and space.

This midweek, mindfulness meditation has changed since its inception. Initially, it unfolded as an opportunity to share practices by key mindfulness practitioners. However, as time passed, it transitioned into something deeper. It became a story within a story and I, as the author, became unknowingly the central character – the constant thread that tied personal stories, insights, mindfulness themes and practices together with a cathartic, self-reflective thread.

My Wise Wife and two daughters, Brown Eyes and Blue Eyes, have emerged as essential secondary characters. I initially adapted these descriptive alias names as a means of protecting their anonymity, but as personal stories and insights emerged, these identities were embraced. I have shared the pleasantness and the unpleasantness of my life's events. The sharing of personal stories and insights has helped me to gain new perspectives, constantly appreciative of those who come in and out of my life, and who have provided me with a fertile ground from which to write.

Years have passed and these writings have inadvertently created a personal memoir. What began as a simple gesture of goodwill has become an unexpected gift to myself, my family, and to my healthcare colleagues. Many of you continue to connect to these weekly mindfulness chronicles and have shared delight in being part of my extended family, feeling like you have gotten to know us weekly while contemplating personal wellbeing, and professional practice. Many have shared with me how they print these personal stories and insights and share them in their workplaces and with family members. Many have written to me on a regular basis to express how these personal stories and insights have resonated, often having lived similar experiences. Some have shared deeply and expressed their gratitude.

I have taught mindfulness meditation since 2009, when I first introduced formal mindfulness practices such as the body scan and awareness of breath to dialysis patients to help relieve their suffering. These patients suffered profoundly. Life sustaining dialysis treatment for persons with end stage renal disease is invasive and disruptive. Jon Kabat-Zinn has referred to hospitals as "dukkha magnets." Dukkha means to suffer. Dialysis units are containers of profound suffering.

In 2012, I implemented a modified version of Mindfulness-Based Stress Reduction programming for health care workers, new nurse graduates, radiation therapy students and leaders in a hospital setting. My wife, also a medical social worker, trained in mindfulness, co-facilitated this with me.

In my quest to embody the practice and ensure that my teaching was authentic, I furthered my training in Mindfulness-Based Stress Reduction. I completed several Mindfulness training opportunities through the Center for Mindfulness in Medicine, Health Care, and Society - University of Massachusetts Medical School, and obtained my qualification to teach in April 2016. I have had the privilege of teaching Mindfulness-Based Stress Reduction to patients and families, healthcare professionals, and to the public. Mindfulness has become an integral part of my life.

I grew up in a small steel town in northeastern Ontario, as a member of a Canadian Italian family with much love and much excitement. My inclination was one of anxiety and reactivity. Mindfulness has helped me to observe my thoughts as just thoughts. Mindfulness provides me with the freedom to govern my life in a more responsive fashion. I learned that I had choice and that there is power in taking a purposeful pause, observing, and then proceeding. I believe that, in order to teach mindfulness, one must embody it. I am aware and awake to the pain, the neutrality, and the beauty of life in all that I do and see. I attend yoga regularly, as well as go to the breath daily. I am fortunate to have a loving partner who also understands the importance of the practice and is a co-teacher of Mindfulness-Based Stress Reduction with me. I live, breathe, and dream mindfulness. My creativity allows me to propose new ideas and I am eager to develop mindfulness opportunities for others. I read about mindfulness daily to keep current with evidence-based studies. I am consulted in my home community and internationally to teach mindfulness key concepts and practices to business professionals, academia, elementary schools, healthcare workers, and others. As part of embodying the practice and maintaining my skills as a mindfulness teacher, I attend mindfulness retreats for self-care and to deepen my practice. These opportunities sustain my practice.

These personal stories and mindfulness insights have helped to identify and manage workplace-related stress, provide evidence of collegial compassionate care, and cultivate personal and professional resilience and renewal. I know this from what my global colleagues have shared. The stories remind us that although we are different, we are all connected. They have fostered the delivery of a more human approach to healthcare through contemplative practice and understand what is important and what is trivial in this play that we call "life."

Jon Kabat-Zinn's seven tenets of mindfulness are intertwined with practices for deep reflection and inward journey. You may wish to read this book in chronological order or turn to the chapter that answers the question: What is called for now in this moment?

I encourage you to make this book your own. Mark it up, write your personal reflections in it, highlight segments of it that call out to you, fold the edges, place mementos in it. My favorite mindfulness books are the ones that I have made my home. They invite me to revisit them over and over again, gaining new insights with each read.

Although this book is written for all, Chapters 16, and 18 may resonate with healthcare providers. Having said this, all of you will have health challenges in life and may appreciate the difference that a mindful caregiver makes to your journey.

Mindfulness can be achieved through both informal and formal practices. Informal practice is simply paying attention to what you are doing when you are doing it, utilizing all of your senses. If you are bathing, this means paying attention to the temperature of the water, feel of the soap on the skin, awareness of the scent, and the sensation of rinsing. If you are eating, this is paying attention to the smell of the food, its textures, the taste of the first bite, the colour of the food, plate, utensils, and intentional awareness of the hands that prepared it and so forth.

Formal mindfulness meditation practices include sitting meditation with awareness of the breath, walking meditation, mindful yoga, and body scan. Sitting meditation is often referred to as the heart of formal practice, pivotal for eliciting stillness and groundedness. When we sit we usually adapt a dignified posture. Sometimes, it is helpful to visualize a string attached to the top of your head keeping you upright, straight, and aligned. The spine is erect, with a natural curve. Hands are resting on the thighs. Arms, and shoulders are relaxed. The chin is slightly tucked and eyelids are half-closed with a soft gaze as if looking through a shear curtain. Your view is translucent and the edges softened. The face and jaw are natural and relaxed. The invitation is to allow the lips to part and the tongue to fall or rest gently on the upper pallet.

When sitting on a cushion, your legs are crossed and hips are positioned higher than the knees. When sitting on a chair, both feet are planted firmly on the floor. The chair, cushion, and floor are providing the body with stability for stillness. The invitation is to focus on the breath, which acts as an anchor to bring you to the present moment when thoughts of the past or future arise. The instruction is to simply notice and accept feelings and thoughts that emerge without judgment, letting go with spaciousness, openness and curiosity. I find it helpful to visualize thoughts as leaves floating down a stream. There it is, there it goes. This practice entails being with pleasant, unpleasant, and neutral thoughts and feelings without favouring one over another. You are simply noticing, or as Jon Kabat-Zinn often states, being with the full catastrophe of life.

My hope is that this book will inspire, connect, and help to reacquaint you to a kinder and more mindful way of being with simple mindfulness practices that can be integrated and embodied into your daily life. This is intended to help you to respond to internal and external life stressors with full presence, self-compassion and confidence.

THE SEVEN TENETS OF MINDFULNESS

Nonjudgment

We continually judge our thoughts, our feelings, and our bodies. Our focus is often on negativity rather than what's positive. We want things to be a certain way and judge if we do not achieve this. In a similar way, we judge others. We have been reared in a society that judges. When we go to the cushion, we also judge our practice. We compare ourselves to others. We judge whether we are doing the practice right or wrong. We may prefer some mindfulness practices while we push others away. However, mindfulness is about being kind to self and paying attention to the present moment purposely without judgement. Mindfulness allows us to step back and observe with openness, spaciousness, and curiosity. This gives us incredible freedom.

Patience

Patience refers to our ability to let things unfold in their own accord without rushing them or wishing for things to be different than they are. We often spend time wanting things to be different. In essence, we wish our life away. We are part of a society that seeks instant gratification. Mindful awareness does not materialize immediately. Mindfulness is cultivated slowly through regular practice and with patience as obstacles arise. Patience is a natural part of the process.

Beginner's mind

Children have the gift of being able to see things from an unbiased point of view. We are able to witness this perspective if we watch them at play. As we grow older and have experiences, we form biases that do not serve us in seeing things as they actually are. We create misconceptions and this limits our ability to see clearly. When stressed, we develop tunnel vision, a narrow way of seeing the world and this causes us to be reactive rather than responsive. When we look at things as if we are seeing them for the very first time, we are able to fully appreciate their splendour in a new way.

Trust

Trust invites us to tune into our own basic goodness and realize that we have the innate capacity to develop awareness through mindfulness practices. Jon Kabat-Zinn often reminds us that there is more right with you than wrong with you. Trusting the Mindfulness-Based Stress Reduction program allows us to have confidence in the process and in the curriculum that has been rigorously studied. Mindfulness entails looking both inward and outward. This means respecting our abilities and limitations without judgment, as well as trusting our ability to ask ourselves "what is called for now?"

Non-Striving

We are so caught up in doing, achieving, fixing, and helping that we forget to simply just be. This is especially difficult as we have been doing for so long. The concept of non-striving is new to us. Mindfulness practice is not goal driven. It is about being with the object of awareness in this moment as it is.

Acceptance

There is a well-known saying that what we resist, persists. Acceptance allows us to be with what is. When we stop trying to push away that which is unpleasant, we suffer less and learn to accept things as they are. This means accepting who we are, and the situation at hand, whether pleasant, unpleasant, or neutral. Acceptance is not about being complacent or allowing ourselves to be taken advantage of. It is about knowing that there are some things that we cannot change.

Letting go

When we let go, we no longer suffer. Letting go represents acceptance that there is an impermanent nature to everything. When we try to hang on, it does not serve us. The same can be said about our meditation practice. When thoughts come or our mind wanders, we acknowledge where it has gone, label it, and bring our awareness back to our breath. This coming back to the breath is not a failure. It is an integral part of our practice.

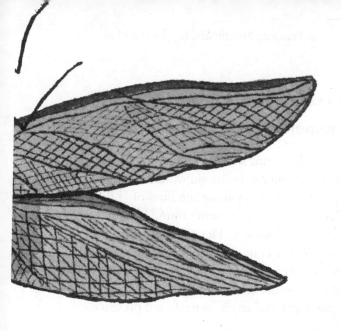

ALL THAT SURROUNDS YOU

We live in a fast-paced world with excessive stimuli and multiple demands, both societal and self-imposed. Although we are more connected than we have ever been with social media and multiple devices, there is a sadness that lurks in the backdrop of this milestone. Rates of depression and anxiety are at record levels. We want to disconnect but our addiction to our mobile phones prevents us from taking a much needed break. It sounds so simple to tell someone to go to the breath or to live in the moment, but to do so is far more complex than this simple well-meaning advice. Loneliness pervades. We don't sleep. We adopt maladaptive coping behaviours to keep afloat, to numb, to avoid, but eventually we get sick emotionally and physically. This chapter represents a humble invitation to simply stop and look with beginners eyes, if even for a moment. We can live robotically in autopilot and miss out on all that surrounds us or we can open our eyes and our hearts and take the time to look. It's all there just waiting for us to notice. We all have the capacity to be mindful.

"Doesn't sound like you are living in the moment Mr. Mindfulness!"

Last night before bed following a full workday, my wife asked me if I had taken time to look out our bedroom window to view the new moon. My retort was something along the lines of "I'll look at it later, thanks." Her response was, "Doesn't sound like you are living in the moment, Mr. Mindfulness." Her rebuttal made me smile. I knew that she was right. I chuckled inside, having been called to task as a mindfulness practitioner and teacher. This gentle nudging invited me to take a moment to look up at the moon, trace its silvery shape with my finger, and enjoy its profound presence.

Practice

» Take a moment today to be truly present. Look into the eyes of that person that sits before you and enjoy the fullness of who they are and what they bring to your day.
» Take a moment tonight to look up to the sky and notice the heavenly bodies.

A canopy of stars

In the summer, I spend time at a cottage on Manitoulin Island, situated in the middle of Lake Huron in Ontario. Imagine the splendour of gazing up at the stars and the rare opportunity to witness the northern lights. Upon spending a night there, I found myself outside looking up to the stars against the stark black backdrop of the endless sky. I felt fortunate to have the opportunity to be in such removed surroundings, away from the city lights and constant array of distractions. I felt privileged to have the gift of vision to see. I felt humbled to be part of something much greater than me.

Practice

- » Find yourself under a canopy of stars. Breathe.
- » Imagine a white ray of light is extending from one of those bright stars.
- » Feel the light pouring on you and entering your body through a small imaginary opening at the top of your head.
- » Allow this white light to scan the body, slowly flowing downwards from your forehead, past your eyelids and to the area of your mouth and jaw. Breathe. Notice.
- » Allow the tongue to fall and relax, the lips to part and the jaw to quiet. Just bask in the gift of this light in quietness.
- » Notice what's there.
- » Now allow the light to flow to your shoulders and neck (often harbouring tension).
- » Let this guiding light flow into your chest, surround your heart and vital organs. Just notice.
- » Follow the white light as it moves to your abdomen and pelvic cavity.
- » Invite it to flow into your arms. Nothing to change or fix.
- » Both legs. Let it settle in your toes.
- » Just allow yourself to be with what is.

Sometimes we simply need to be awakened to life in order to navigate a pathway of living

We sat side by side in a large medical clinic waiting area with paper numbers in hand and the television blaring in the backdrop. Not a word ensued. Many on smartphones, ill, aloof, and indifferent. Then a little girl and her father entered the room. She carried with her a helium filled balloon, and she and the balloon were both bursting at the seams, excited to demonstrate its floating capabilities. Suddenly, there was a huge explosion as the balloon rubbed against the ceiling, likely against something sharp. We all jumped, looked around trying to figure it out and then burst into laughter. We scurried around the little girl to help settle her as she was unhappy. We engaged in conversation, cell phones disappeared and we shared stories of who we were and what had brought us here on this day. Sometimes, we simply need to be awakened to life in order to navigate a pathway of living. Wake up, my friends, wake up!

Practice

» Stop and check in.
» Are you simply going through the motions?
» Do you long for more?
» Put down your mobile devices. Pay attention to those around you and talk to each other.
» Appreciate that your paths may never cross again. Wake up.

It's all there

It's all there. All you have to do is open your eyes to see it. Sitting in the back yard and looking up to the sky. Poplar leaves catching the evening's last rays of sunshine. Millions of white dandelion seeds dancing in the air. The sound of a chirping sparrow curiously frolicking in the garden. The sound of the mourning doves cooing in the backdrop. The coolness of the breeze after a day of warmth. The gardens abloom with iris, azalea, and lily.

Practice

»   Take a few moments to use all of your senses to simply notice.
»   Be aware that misperceptions and habitual reactions erode our ability to see clearly.
»   Bask in all that surrounds you.

The "Hugging Tree"

Week after week, for many years, I have run mindlessly from point A to point B along a meandering pathway that hugs the shoreline of a city park. But even with my running steps in autopilot, I have been drawn to a tree that seems to call to me. This is not an ordinary tree. Its roots cascade into the sandy soil beneath, seemingly clinging for dear life. Its branches stretch outward and upright. I have watched it through all seasons, year after year, with leaves and without leaves, in constant change. It never moves or sways and always looks strong and inviting. I refer to it as "the hugging tree" as it openly extends outward, inviting those that pass to climb up on it and be held.

Practice

» When you find yourself overwhelmed, struggling to stay afloat, stop for a moment and turn to the breath.
» Feel your feet firmly planted, rooted, steady. Breathe.
» Know that, like "the hugging tree," that you too have the capacity to weather change with open arms.

Running centre pavement

Every so often, I have the opportunity to run centre pavement, hitting the surface below me with each striking step, looking aimlessly at the white painted fragmented line. Sometimes, I wonder if this pathway signifies a new opportunity on the horizon, staring me in the face, right before me, but just not clear enough to see. I always view these running opportunities as an invitation to look deeper beneath the surface, beyond monotony and with open curiosity.

Practice

» Let this be your reminder to use your innate mindful awareness to look beneath the surface on which you run daily.
» Pause, breathe and look deeper.
» Be open to where it leads you.

Open your heart and bask in the glow

Recently, I received two strings of multicoloured translucent patio lanterns that I have strung on the arbor of our back deck. The rays of the sun power these solar marvels have conjured fond memories of my early years. As a child, my family and I embarked on many camping excursions. The campsite would be set up, the fire prepared and the plastic multicoloured patio lanterns would be strewn to act as a beacon of light. We would sit by the fire until we could no longer keep our eyes open, and then head to bed for rest. The transparent fabric of the tent would allow for light to shine through, shimmering orange from the glow of the fire and a multitude of colours from the patio lanterns. Life seemed so simple back then. I would just lie there, listening to the lull of chatter, the crackle of fire and the gift of being in the moment. Eventually, the fire would reduce to ashes and voices would fade. If one got up in the middle of the night, the eye would see nothing but patio lanterns and millions of stars for miles.

Practice

> » Take a moment to open your hearts today and bask in the glow.
> » Let the awareness that is cultivated through the practice of mindfulness illuminate your journey in all that you say and do.
> » Know that your inner wisdom and clarity will bring you comfort in times of darkness.

Ebb and flow

One day seems to blend into the next like the palate of colours that grace each vivid sunrise and sunset. The birds start their unrelenting chorus at about 4:30 a.m. Beanie bag goes into the microwave and the coffee brews at 5:45 a.m. Shoes are laced at 7:20 a.m. We begin our familiar walk to work. First sighting of Queen Anne's Lace offers anticipation of upcoming holidays and cottage escapades due to arrive soon. Workday begins at 8:00 a.m. and story after story continues to unfold until 4:00 p.m. when I dash out. Home, dinner, the events of the evening, and then to bed. The cycle repeats itself again and again. Like ebb and flow on the ocean, dawn becomes dusk, crescent moon swells to full moon and we immerse ourselves in this rhythmical way of being. Life is good.

Practice

- » Pay attention to all that surrounds you.
- » Stop. Breathe. Notice these cyclical patterns, your habitual patterns and behaviours.
- » Understand that you have choice.

Snow white quartz envelops my body

The snow-white quartz envelops my body, like crispy white sun-bleached sheets. It molds to all crevices of my silhouette, suspends me, grounds me, and engulfs me in this place somewhere between where I was and where I hope to be. Laying beneath the dancing pines that desperately cling to barren rock, the August sun warms me and reaffirms my appreciation of this moment. I am so pleased to be here. Now, today!

Practice

- » The next time you are feeling worried or anxious you may wish to use this mindfulness visualization to ground you and bring you back to this moment.
- » Find a place where you can lay on your back safely.
- » Use this time to gently explore the sensations in your body, scanning sequentially from head to toe, just checking in.
- » This might be a gentle way of waking up in the morning and setting the stage for how your day will unfold.

Catch a dancing leaf mindfully

My dentist's office is situated in a glass tower that overlooks an expansive concrete parking lot bordered by walls of adjacent downtown buildings. Some old with character, and some new and modern, but all devoid of warmth or feeling. I was there once again for required dental work.

My dentist left the room for the freezing to take hold, so I found myself curiously staring out the window. Then suddenly I had a mindful moment! In this sea of concrete, my eyes were suddenly drawn to a large oak leaf that appeared from nowhere, aimlessly floating about, journeying with the wind as its navigator.

To my amazement, the wind whisked the leaf from floating and made it dance. Just when I thought it might disappear out of sight, the wind would magically grab a hold of it and snag it back within my view. This went on for just a minute, but during that time I was entirely focused on the present moment, not preoccupied with what was to come nor thinking about the events that had transpired. That dentist appointment and cold concrete backdrop served up a venue of awareness and awe. In the experience of unpleasantness, I was open to experience a pleasant moment. This was mindfulness at its best.

Practice

» Soften your gaze and take a few deep breaths.
» Visualize catching that leaf as it floats past your viewpoint.
» Simply be with it .... feeling the texture .... focusing on the shape and colour.
» With your fingertip, gently trace the periphery of it.
» Imagine holding it up to the light and looking at the translucence of it.
» Look a bit further to the veins and junctures.
» With openness and spaciousness, look to where it has been and to where it is going with no expectations.
» Enjoy.

A world defined with clarity, vision, and retrospection

Despite the cold weather, I still headed out for my morning run before sunrise. I put on another layer of clothing to combat the frigid temperatures and headed out the door. It was one of those mornings when I questioned the entire act of running. Did I really need to do this? Wouldn't it have been nicer to just stay in bed a bit longer? Was it just too cold to go out and should my body have a well-deserved rest today?

Yet, shutting the door was like entering a new world. A world defined with clarity, vision, and retrospection. I looked up to the sky and it was inundated with a thousand stars and a crescent moon. The sunrise was on the horizon inviting me to savour the day. The water in the distance was mirror-like, inviting personal reflection and hope.

In essence, the practice of mindfulness invites us to open the door and enter such a world every time we go to the cushion. Like the stars that are always above us, we forget to be present in the moment, yet the moment is always there to enjoy if we open ourselves up to it.

Practice

- » Pause. Breathe. Reflect.
- » Take a moment today. Soften your gaze. Open your heart, and dedicate some quiet time to just be.
- » If you find yourself making excuses to not practise your meditation, go to the cushion if even for a short time.

Mapping out pathways

We had been hit with our first significant snowfall of the season. Mother Nature unsympathetically dumped half a foot of snow upon us as we slept, tucked safety beneath our sheets. My initial intention was to simply get myself to work and luckily, I live close enough that I could walk. At the end of my work day, I realized I would be facing a snow-filled driveway. The snow plough had cordoned off my driveway with a two-foot wall fortress of white. The temperature was pleasant. The snow light and buoyant. What began as a painstaking task became pleasurable. I absorbed the solace. I caught up with some neighbours. I reminisced about being a child and bolting out the door after each snowstorm determined to launch my snow shoveling entrepreneurship. I mindfully walked up and down the driveway carving out lines, shuffling through snow, allowing for my feet to caress the earth aimlessly.

Practice

» Arrive wherever you are with curiosity, play, and open eyes.
» Trust in your inner wisdom to shovel through life's chaos, pain, and suffering.
» Don't allow your thoughts to become fortresses that seem impermeable.

Airports

I find airports to be fascinating spaces. They are pivotal transition points that represent either the end of a journey or the beginning. They are places where hours and hours of time pass just sitting, captive. If we open our eyes, we may notice that they are more than just waiting spaces. They are filled with lovers saying hello and goodbye, families receiving or sending off children, parents, and relatives and lone travellers. Like airports, there are times in our life when we may feel stuck in circumstances completely out of our control. This may include being caught in a traffic jam, being on hold during a phone call, or finding ourselves in a line up at a coffee shop. If we pause, breathe and pay purposeful attention we can begin to feel more present. Presence puts us in control.

Practice

» Check in rather than check out.

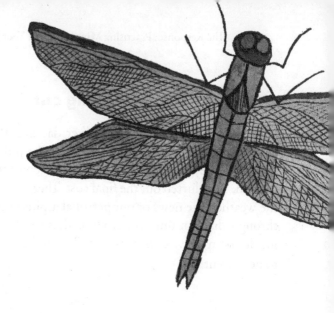

- 2 -

THE GIFT OF THE BREATH

Why is it that we neglect to fully appreciate all that we have until it is at risk? We usually go about our day – doing, fixing, accomplishing, and consequently in this way of going through the motions, we miss out, make mistakes, and feel unhappy. The act of pausing and directing your awareness to the breath is singlehandedly one of the most important gifts that you can give to yourself. This anchors us to the present moment, allows us to take inventory of our thoughts, feelings, bodies and proceed with wisdom. Life is hard. Going to breath offers us the opportunity to know that we can ride the ebb and flow of life, breath by breath without suffocating in the process. This, in turn, offers us hope.

Checking out

I was in the supermarket the other day and the checkout clerk whisked my groceries through quickly. She did not connect with me through eye contact. She made no attempt to converse and, in the end, she blurted out the final cost. There was no dialogue about the weather, the news or our personal aspirations. We simply went through the motions. The irony is that there was no one behind me. It doesn't have to be this way. We can slow down and take time to be present.

Practice

» Take five minutes today from your busy schedule to breathe.
» Be with all those who you interact with today.
» Look in their eyes. Listen to them as they tell their story. Be kind and curious.
» Avoid the default mode of simply checking out.

The art of scraping by

At the end of our workday and after a cold walk home, we delighted in a black bean cheddar quinoa casserole. As my Wise Wife scraped her plate of melted cheese and other tantalizing remnants, I shared with her that I had absolutely no idea what I was going to write about for this week's meditation blog. Like the ringing of the gong that echoed an hour earlier at meditation class, my writer's block suddenly dissipated and thoughts reverberated.

The scraping of the plate triggered me to think of how many of us often just scrape by desperately clinging to future hopes and aspirations, inadvertently wishing our lives away. Our remnants often include loss, body change and self-blame. Like the gift of the breath, we take the gift of our body for granted.

Practice

- » Take a few moments out of your busy workday to simply go to the breath and be aware.
- » Realize that you have choice.
- » You can just scrape by in autopilot or you can make your day count!

Foreign but so familiar

Treading through parkland, covered with a fresh blanket of snow, I noticed something motorized with flashing lights flying above me. It seemed so out of place in this quiet space, foreign but familiar. I could hear the engine noise as this plane floated above me, reminding me of the foreign yet familiar relationship that we have with the breath. Breathe, feel, see.

Practice

- » Throughout your day, pause and simply take a moment to acknowledge the breath.
- » Look for its familiar qualities.
- » Look for its unfamiliar qualities.
- » Then, be with it.

Achoo

Walking through the medical unit yesterday, I was overtaken by a sequence of four loud sneezes. Each sneeze initiated automatic responses from others uttering the response of "bless you." One patient told staff that each sneeze represented the soul leaving the body and being sent back from heaven. This resonated with me throughout the day. I began to think of this concept metaphorically and its similarity to the significance of returning to the breath when your mind is carried away by rumination. Air is channeled out of our body, sent to the universe, purified, only to be breathed back to the body. And with each in-breath comes the opportunity to begin again. The two words begin again are two of the most significant words in the practice of mindfulness. The invitation to begin again builds on the skills that you have developed in your meditation practice. Begin again offers hope that you can get beyond some of the common obstacles in meditation – boredom, monkey mind, and body discomfort by simply returning to the breath.

Practice

»   Realize that every breath that you take today allows for you to begin again.
»   Know that, in your meditation practice, that your mind will wander.
»   When this happens gently and firmly bring your awareness back to the breath.

A gift to be celebrated

If everywhere I look is so beautiful, how can I be miserable?

The trees are profuse with blossoms. The flowers are emerging from the earth. The lakes echo deep blue, new green reflections and an abundance of life. The lawns are lush green, dotted with yellow dandelions. The problem is...I can't breathe. Pollen covers everything with a chartreuse layer of residue that blankets all. With seasonal allergies, my immune system is in full tilt and this leaves me feeling tired and depleted by day's end. We often take the breath for granted. As part of our autonomic nervous system, the breath seldom gets the attention and appreciation that it deserves. It is a gift to be honoured and celebrated, one breath at a time.

Practice

» Practise abdominal breathing by laying down flat on your back, or with your feet resting elevated on a chair in an astronaut pose.
» Place your hands on your belly .
» Notice its rising and falling with the in-breath and the out-breath.
» Observe your breathing from moment to moment.
» Bring your attention back to the breath and the present moment when your mind wanders.

New pathways

I rode my bicycle to work today for the first time this season. Dodging traffic, this awakened my attention to the surroundings of spring and allowed for my auditory senses to delight in the sound of robins, new leaves rustling in the wind, and the distant sound of children playing from sunlight to sunset. Like a young explorer, I veered off the beaten path, taking side streets that I hadn't navigated previously.

Riding a bicycle, once learned, becomes instinctual. In many ways it is similar to our innate ability to return to the breath. When we practise mindfulness meditation, we mount our seat, put the palms of our hands on our thighs (like we did when we fearlessly rode our bicycles with no hands!), and we embrace the moment. It is normal for our minds to wander down alternate pathways but gently bringing our awareness back to the breath will help us to navigate the journey. Today, I wish for you butterfly handlebars with streamers, a psychedelic banana seat and lots of hands-free sailing.

Practice

» Be a mindful explorer today.
» Play, be curious, and veer off your beaten path.
» Return to the breath at any time if feeling overwhelmed.

An old friend who has always been

Why must everything be so complicated? If you wish to purchase an item, there are usually so many varieties that the task can be daunting. Food items are the same with a choice of organic, farm fed, pesticide-free, not genetically altered, hybrids, and so on.

When we look at the practice of mindfulness, we often make things much more difficult than they have to be. No matter what challenges we face in the day, a return to the breath allows for grounding and replenishment. When I teach people formal mindfulness meditation practice, I usually encourage them to welcome the gift of the breath like an old friend who has always been with them. I invite them to open their awareness to the breath, without over-analyzing it or striving to make it different. This act of kindness to self is both simple and profound.

Practice

> » Take some time from your busy day to get reacquainted with that old friend, the breath. Simple but unfaltering.

Refuge

She sat across from me and spoke of her past year. Difficulty in accepting traumatic events that unfolded, she spoke of how the practice of going to the breath, a mindfulness practice, has become her refuge – like coming home. I knew what she meant. We all need a place that will offer us comfort and time out. Take a moment to find refuge by going to the breath during those trying times in your life. Stress is often referred to as our inability to deal with challenges that exceed our inner resources. Stress may be related to an unhealthy workplace, life passages, loss, finances, or change.

Practice

> » Cue into your thoughts, emotions and body sensations.
> » Notice where you hold tightness or stiffness in your body.
> » Recognize this tension as an indicator that it's time to go to silence.
> » Take refuge.

A friend within

I received an unexpected telephone call from my friend Stan after a busy, mundane work day. My mind was stuck in the January blahs and longing for spring, sunshine, and warmth.

Stan and I have been friends for 38 years. Although we reside in different cities, have different occupations, our own families and new acquaintances, there is an instinctive connection that comforts and invokes laughter, reminiscence, and emotion when we reconnect. It is hard to imagine that we were the same young teens who drove up and down Queen Street in Sault Ste. Marie, Ontario, listening to the music of the early 1970's in Stan's old burgundy Acadian, eons ago but seemingly just like yesterday.

Stan was the Ukrainian boy who flew paper planes over my head in math class in a small steel-town high school and who stood out amongst my Italian friends with funny names with rhythmic syllables. Today, we enjoy a mutual passion for running that has awakened our souls and now connects us by the gift of movement. Stan is also a helping professional; he is a firefighter. Although different, we are also connected in this regard. As a healthcare professional, I too feel like I am constantly putting out fires. Fires that destroy spirit, erode hope, and deplete one's "being."

We all have a friend within us that offers us the opportunity to re-connect. The name of this friend is "the breath" and it has been with us since the day we were born. It knows our strengths and our idiosyncrasies. It has the potential to calm, awaken or empower. It too can ground us and keep us resilient.

Practice

» Take a few moments to re-connect with your friend – "the breath."

» Put your thoughts and work demands aside, and allow yourself to be open to receive the call from your old friend.

The bus

As I walked to work, a tall, gangly young red headed teen almost ran me off the pathway. As usual he was headed towards his school bus pick up. Each day, I delight in watching this teenager gingerly prance by, grasping his books and school bag. I delight in watching the bus pull up and his successful conquest of it at the very last minute. I marvel at his agility and admire his ability to sleep to the last minute and then make it to school on time. We often go through life running. Sometimes, we just make it. Sometimes, we miss the bus entirely. The practice of mindfulness can be a chance to breathe and slow things down. When we do this, we can suppress our sympathetic nervous system. The sympathetic nervous system is part of our autonomic nervous system, the part that kicks in when we are under stress and ignites our fight, flight, freeze response. This helps us to simply feel better.

Practice

» Pause, walk, breathe...don't run.

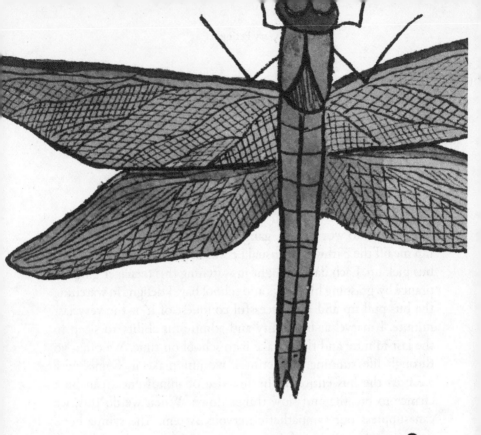

THOSE WHO SHARE YOUR PATH

It is easy to judge. We often have misperceptions of others based on our previous experiences and biases. Sometimes, we are just too tired to put forth the effort required to connect with others. It is so much easier on an elevator or in a busy waiting room to pick up our mobile phone and not engage or have eye contact. We have choice though. We can go through the motions or we can be open to all those who share our path. These strangers who share our path have a lot to teach us if we are receptive, open minded and curious. Mindfulness helps us to welcome all.

Fully present

I love Sundays. I wake up at the crack of dawn, have my warm cup of coffee, don my running gear and head for the road. My eldest daughter, Blue Eyes, has witnessed this phenomenon. I believe her words echoed something like "Oh dad, running tights, orange jacket and small bright red back pack...how embarrassing!" So, this past Christmas, she equipped me with a new running backpack to assist me with my weekly excursion. My destination: a local bakery six kilometres away from my home. I turn up my music, set my GPS, mesmerized by rocky landscapes and frozen lakes, and catch snowflakes with my tongue.

This Sunday, I noticed something different. As I ran through the downtown core past the soup kitchen, my eyes were met with the eyes of a stranger, shivering in the cold – glassy. They reached out to my soul. I ran past with an uncomfortable feeling that gnawed at my belly. I did hit the bakery, but I could not get the lingering image of those eyes to dissipate.

I then made a conscious decision to purchase a second loaf of fresh hot bread for this person as a gesture of good will. I filled my backpack with bread and croissants and made a brief stop at the soup kitchen, offering the loaf to my new friend before departing.

Practice

» When you are rushing past a stranger today, pause, look into their eyes.
» Allow yourself to be fully present.
» Drop judgment.
» Be compassionate.

Each of us comes with our own cover letter

Sitting after dinner, my youngest daughter, Brown Eyes, shared with me her cover letter as she is soon to graduate from university and will be entering the job market. It is hard to believe that the little girl, who I followed on a bus to assure her safe arrival on the first day of school, has developed into a fine young woman with an impressive summary of accomplishments. This string of achievements paints a picture and sets the stage for the next part of her journey. A coming to be.

Each of us has a cover letter or a storyline that depicts who we are and where we have come from. It pays tribute to our accomplishments and it celebrates who we have become. But paper deteriorates and ink fades. It will be the interactions we have with people on a daily basis that will make the most significant impressions. When we are mindful, our interpersonal skills are enhanced. We are more responsive and less reactive. We listen more attentively, and we speak more wisely. We also care more deeply.

Practice

» Bring your awareness to your daily interactions.
» Acknowledge that we all have storylines.
» Be kind.

Just like the Craigslist did for Joe

I watched the documentary, Craigslist Joe, and felt inspired by the story. The premise of the movie is the world is full of compassionate people who are interconnected and totally accessible via Craigslist, an American classified advertisements website. The main character, Joe, leaves behind his family, friends and job to see if he can survive solely on the support and goodwill of others, and he does so by accessing Craigslist for employment, food, accommodation, haircuts and anything else he requires to survive. Upon his return home, at the end of the movie, he reflects on this experience and how the people he met along the way profoundly changed his life.

This made me think of how lucky we are to meet such wonderful and diverse people in our daily lives. I am amazed at the unfolding that occurs as we sit across from strangers who enter our space and share the intimacy of their lives. In essence, their rich storyline deeply influences us.

In in my work as a social worker, I have met a gifted musician, an escort service provider, a person with schizophrenia and a person adverse to change. Being mindful is pivotal in moving us from empathy to compassion. When we are compassionate, we are motivated by a desire to understand and respond. Mindfulness connects us, just like the Craigslist did for Joe.

Practice

> » When you feel separate, bring your awareness to the threads that connect us to others.

She magically pivots her dust mop beneath swivel chairs

We have a custodian who helps us keep order in the hospital. She arrives at about 2:30 p.m. and works late into the night. The sound of her yellow cleaning cart makes its distinct rumbling sound to announce her arrival. She is a very talkative, gentle soul with razor sharp intuitive skills, who takes delight in her work and often comes bearing candy to share. She takes tremendous pride in her work. She gently reminds you when you are working too hard and, in her own motherly way, suggests the need for self-care. She gently whisks her damp cloth across desks, respectful of all the clutter. She magically pivots her dust mop beneath swivel chairs and manages to tell you about the weather, world events, and the latest hockey game scores in the process.

Practice

» Take some time, today, to reflect on the special people that are in your workplace and who grace your life.
» Recognize how we rely on one another.

When pain comes knocking at our door

I sat across from a young man, today, who was referred to me for non-adherence to his medical regime. He sat quietly as if he had been escorted to the principal's office, sitting upright, head looking downward, sad eyes poking through locks of dark brown unruly curls, tears streaming from his eyes. I made my inquiries balanced with kindness, and he told me his story.

The pain he described was jagged and intense. An abrupt change in his family circumstances had caught him completely by surprise. His pain produced feelings of numbness to his outer world and tightness that made it difficult for him to catch his breath in between sentences. This unexpected life interruption was both profound and piercing. Acute. I felt humbled to be in his presence.

Mindfulness helps us to look at pain with openness and curiosity while not being consumed by it. Pain comes knocking at our door, pulls up a chair and visits when we least expect it. When we allow it to enter, we welcome all that it has to teach us in the moment.

Practice

» Acknowledge pain when it comes knocking at your door.
» Don't run from it.
» Be with it.
» Realize its fluidity.
» Let it be your teacher.

I wanted to say

I wanted to say to my physician today, "I'm so sorry about the loss of your mother," but something held me back. I wanted to say, this morning, to my colleagues, "just knock it off and be reasonable," but something held me back. I wanted to say to a patient, yesterday, "come on, do something, you're killing yourself slowly," but something held me back. That something sits on your shoulder. It imposes social constructs and limits your ability to be authentic.

It sometimes precludes the ability to speak out forthright amidst societal nuances. Mindfulness helps one to pause, take a breath, observe, and proceed. We learn when to speak and when not to.

Practice

> » Bring your awareness to those times when you want to say something.
> » Before you do, check in with self.
> » Only proceed when you feel it is right to do so.

Faces

We really are creatures of habit. I walk to work daily, following the same route, crossing the lights at the same places, and cutting through the same path. I could probably do this with my eyes shut but then I would miss all of those beautiful faces that I meet on my daily route.

There is the coffee slinger. She walks holding onto her coffee cup for dear life. It is one of those large thermos cups. She swigs sips, smiling and exchanging a good morning. There are the two young teenaged boys, both swinging their gym bags and enthralled in conversation. They are comrades. There is the bigger burly older teen with hoodie up, head down, no smile and seemingly carrying the weight of the world on his shoulders, and there is the young girl with piercing blue eyes.

Practice

> » We all experience sadness or loneliness, and we all want to belong. We all have hopes and dreams. We all wish to be loved.
> » Take a few moments in your autopilot routine, today, to simply notice faces.
> » Notice the faces of those people in your life who love you, or whom you love dearly.
> » Notice the faces of strangers, people who you do not know but perhaps would like to.
> » Notice the faces of those persons in your life who you find difficult.
> » Then look into the mirror and notice your face.
> » Now open your heart and wish all loving kindness, and that includes you.

Pause and see

He passed me on his bicycle, and then looked back and grinned. Spring has finally arrived and it looked to me like it was this young boy's first ride of the season. He looked so proud, carefree and excited. I would have missed it had I not been paying attention. I was mesmerized by his self-assured smile and the twinkle in his eyes that said to me that he was wise beyond his years.

Practice

> » In your haste, today, take a moment to pause and look back.
> » Don't miss out on all that the world can teach if we just take the time to look.
> » Take time to pause and see.
> » Really see.

We all take pathways

We all take pathways. The pathways can be direct and uneventful or they can be dotted along the way with smiles, nods, well wishes or eyes cast down to the pavement. Sometimes, the pathways are external leading from one destination to another. Sometimes, they are internal with many of us striving to get somewhere else emotionally and spiritually. Sometimes, there is a sense of deep connection with the gift of a companion walking the path beside you. Sometimes, the path is frightening and lonely, and you just want to turn back. At times, the pathways are manmade, dictated by rules or policies that don't seem to make any sense. At times, they are filled with acronyms and forced with the artificial tracing of complex algorithms that make you feel lost or inadequate. At times, the pathway is created to achieve a goal, but with further exploration, the goal is unclear or perhaps it is someone else's goal that may be less honourable than your own.

Practice

> » Set an intention.
> » Be authentic along your pathway.
> » Make sure to keep your eyes, ears, and heart open along the way.
> » When you get off track, or it doesn't feel right, pause, breathe, and recalculate.

Hope

A morning run amidst a grey angry sky, and as I glanced into the distance, there was a tiny drop of vivid pink that invited the eye and seemed to yell "hope." This made me think of a patient I worked with recently. He sat motionless, hooked up to a machine like it was an extension of his body, an unwelcomed guest. The nurse summoned me to try to calm him. The smell of urea permeated the air. The patient wept quietly. I held his hand, and together, we sat in silence. What could I possibly say or do to make this new dialysis experience palatable?

Months later, this same patient shared with me that my presence made a huge difference in his ability to get through those first days on treatment. Puzzled, I asked how I did this. "You told me I would be okay and you gave me hope," he shared. All of us have the capacity to offer hope. We all have the potential to offer a glimmer of colour amidst a grey sky.

Practice

» When you find yourself slipping into darkness check in. Breathe.

» What is happening in your thoughts, body sensations, and emotions?

» Anchor yourself to the present moment.

» Notice what you know and what you don't know about the situation.

» Notice how easy it is to allow negativity to be your default mode.

» Remind yourself of times in your life when you have worried and your worries have not materialized.

» Proceed with hope.

Compassionate inquiry

It was a rainy day and I decided to walk to work, taking my umbrella and chance-it with the weather. I made some stops along the way and then started to navigate across a very busy intersection. Rather than put myself in danger and cross in a haphazardous fashion, I proceeded to the traffic lights and pressed the walk button, waiting for the light to signify that it was safe to proceed and then heading across the intersection. Half way across, a car spun around the corner turning left and raced towards me. The driver slammed on the brakes and the vehicle slid towards me. I felt it nudge up against my leg as I jumped up in the air to dodge it. I looked at the driver, a young man in his thirties, sporting a dark beard and glasses, and as his eyes met mine, I saw fear. In those few seconds, when the car was heading towards me, I thought, so this is it...this is how I am going to die. Then the driver spun off in the other direction.

I was visibly shaken and I could see that onlookers were also shocked with what they had just witnessed. For me, the most troubling part of the experience was no one stopped to ask if I was okay. I kept walking and looking back, hopeful that the driver might feel some sense of remorse and apologize, but none came.

Part of me was thankful to be alive and part of me was angry. I asked myself, how could this driver not see me? I was carrying my very large, bright green and orange plaid umbrella. As I reflected on the experience, it dawned on me that the driver was an example of someone living life mindlessly. He was rushing in autopilot trying to get somewhere to do something that he may have perceived as important, and he was oblivious to me and my umbrella.

This incident reminded me to not waste life living in autopilot and missing out on the world. It also reminded me to take time to genuinely be present with others.

Practice

> » Being present means mindfully inquiring as to the well-being of one another with compassion, genuineness, and presence.
> » Take a moment today to ask a friend, loved one or stranger... "how are you doing?"

She was human

She entered my office bent over and clasping her handbags. She took the chair directly across from me and looked me in the eyes. She was clear with what she wanted and why she had come to see me. She spoke about attending a mental health group in the community but told me she did not see the point as they were not allowed to talk about trauma. She stated "Doesn't everyone have trauma in their life – what are we supposed to talk about then?" She made raw sense. She used obscenities more than once and spoke of her desire to attend my upcoming Mindfulness-Based Stress Reduction Program. She was seeking help to manage her pain and to quiet her ruminating mind. There was something refreshingly authentic about her amidst her squirming, cursing, and candour. She was human.

Practice

> » Drop your storylines, today, and be your authentic self.
> » Drop expectations, misperceptions, and judgment.
> » Be human.

Compassion for self

The Northern Ontario School of Medicine's curriculum for physicians-in-training includes interacting with allied health professionals in frontline practice. As a preceptor, a first-year medical student shadowed me in an effort to learn more about my work as a medical social worker. She was as young as my daughter and had an insatiable thirst for as much knowledge as she could attain. We discussed the chronicity of the patients, the impact of disease on the family, and I cited many interesting patient experiences. I believe that I offered all of the underpinnings necessary for her to understand the complexity of my work.

Then it dawned on me that I had neglected to share with her the most vital piece of advice. An opportunity to meditate with a client reminded me to delve into the topic of self-care for the practitioner. I stressed the importance of "finding balance in one's life" that might include a routine of yoga, running or meditation. It might also simply include leaving your desk at noon to go and eat your lunch away from your never-ending pile of things to do.

My hope is that, in twenty years, our paths will cross again and this medical student will recall this day as a juncture that defined who she has become – a confident and skilled physician, who has compassion towards others but most importantly who has compassion for self.

Practice

>   » Take a moment to open up your calendar, pause, and just be with it.
>   » How does it make you feel when you stop long enough to see it?
>   » What is happening in your thoughts, emotions, and body?

» Ask yourself "is there balance?"
» Proceed with clarity and wisdom.
» Realize that you have choice.

Buddha's belly

He was my last appointment of the day. I reviewed his medical chart and anticipated that he would not show. Part of me hoped that he would attend and part of me hoped that he would not. I was fatigued and saturated by the week's end. But when I checked the waiting room, twenty-five minutes after his due-to-arrive time, he was there and looked up under long wispy hair. He smiled and followed me to my office.

He was a young man, somewhat introverted but articulate in telling me his story. He had endured tremendous suffering in his life. During the conversation, he spotted a small ivory Buddha figurine sitting on my desk. He asked if he could touch the Buddha's belly and I slid it near him.

He shared a legend derived from the Chinese proverb of the laughing Buddha that suggests that if one rubs the Buddha's belly, it brings forth wealth, good luck, and prosperity. This is exactly what this patient offered me today. He touched me with his presence. He helped me to appreciate how insignificant my problems were and he helped me to appreciate the wealth that I have in all domains of my life.

Practice

» Lay on your back and place your hands on your belly.
» Take a few moments to simply feel the in-breath and the out-breath.
» Be grateful.

Except for her

For three days in a row I have witnessed her. On the weekend, I altered my running route. I decided that a detour through a walkway that floats on top of a marsh might be a welcomed change. The walkway is made of cedar planks and sits adjacent to millions of cattails, lily pads and is filled with sightings of Baltimore Orioles. Each footstep seems magical. The pathway is empty, like a secret passage that has not yet been discovered by others. Except for her.

She walks slowly back and forth, dressed in a long winter-white coat. Her head is covered with matching fabric. Her face is aged, beautiful. She smiles. Her camera is set up on a tripod she is maneuvering. We don't say any words to each other, but I know that she too sees the magic that I see. I glide passed her, surprisingly comforted by her presence.

Practice

» Take a detour today.
» Open your eyes and look for her.

A special visitor

I parked my car, put my headphones on, as I do most days, and began my walk to work. It was a typical late October frost-tinged morning. This daily ritualistic walk entails passing by a large urban park adjacent to a lake with hills, and colourful foliage dotting the landscape.

It was then, from out of the blue, that a young boy about twelve years old, came sailing by on a bicycle. Beyond the sound of my music, I soon realized that he was making a concerted effort to win my attention by mouthing some words that were, at first, incomprehensible. Rather than ignore him, I took off my ear buds and made myself present to the moment.First, he wished me a good morning. He then proceeded to describe his bicycle escapades. His cheeks were rosy, eyes were full of life and voice was filled with passion about cycling and life in general. This young lad then demonstrated his agility by balancing himself like a human elastic band, standing up on his crossbar, sitting on his handle bars, and standing on his seat. I began to sound like an overprotective parent, encouraging my new friend to be careful. This special visitor followed me for some time. He asked me where I went to school and I shared my education history. I told him about my work at the hospital, the inner dealings of the body, where I park my car and walk from daily, and how I ended up living in Sudbury. I shared what music I was listening to on my headphones.

This whole event uplifted my soul and was the best part of my day. This was an extraordinary opportunity to truly be mindful of the moment.

Practice

- » Take a couple of moments, wherever you are, to truly be open to the moment.
- » You could do this formally through sitting mindfulness meditation or you can playfully immerse yourself in the moment, doing the task at hand.
- » Be open to your special visitor!

The brave among us

There is an older gentleman who walks in our neighbourhood. I often see him with his cane, slowly navigating his way down an incline, usually as I am finishing up my morning run. He wears a tweed English cap and is dressed meticulously. His face is weathered, bearded and his smile subdued but apparent. I marvel at his perseverance and brave example.

We are surrounded by many brave people in our lives who navigate through all that life sends their way. Sometimes, composed and well put together. Other times tired-looking and disheveled. A senior persevering through health challenges, a mother adjusting to a new baby, a firefighter saving lives. They appear in many variations. If we open our eyes, without forming opinions, and drop our bias, we can learn so much from their fearlessness.

Practice

> » Be aware of brave people that you see during your day.
> » Notice your preconceived ideas or judgments.
> » Be open to their life lessons.

PHD

Many of us understand the metaphor of putting on our own oxygen mask first before we can effectively care for others. We all need people in our lives who will listen, validate what we are feeling, and provide honest feedback. Sometimes, this is the first step in helping us to look at our situation and realize that there needs to be change.

My PHD – "professional hair dresser" – Cavelle listens with true presence, demonstrates non-judgment, is compassionate, and offers a hug upon completion of each hair appointment. We leave every visit feeling more optimistic and our problems feel more manageable.

Practice

- » P- pause
- » H- be aware of habitual reactions
- » D- decide to respond, rather than react

A complete turnaround

After December 21, there is more light than darkness. It is a complete turnaround, a solstice. In the early morning darkness, I began my run. We had a fresh snowfall so pathways were snow covered camouflaging a layer of black ice. I vacillated between whether I should go out given the weather conditions or skip the run altogether. In the end, the run won out and I decided to brave the elements.

I have run for seventeen years in the winter and fortunately only fallen once. This day marked my second fall. With music blasting from my earbuds, I suddenly lost my footing and landed flat on my back, belly up. As I looked upward in bewilderment, I was face to face with a man who was peering down at me in astonishment.

He asked if I was okay. He reached out his arm to help me up. He cautioned that the pathways were slippery and suggested the need for me to be more careful. He was a compassionate soul who in that moment seemed to feel my pain and genuinely wanted to help. But there was a familiarity about his face. I recognized him but could not place who he was.

Eventually it came to me that he was a former kidney transplant patient from many years ago. Like the shift from darkness to light, it dawned on me that the shoe was on the other foot this time. An eye opener. A complete turnaround.

Practice

» Bring your awareness to a time in your life when you lost your footing.
» What was happening in your thoughts, feelings and body?
» Bring your awareness to someone who may be struggling today.
» Extend a helping hand to them without expectation or judgement

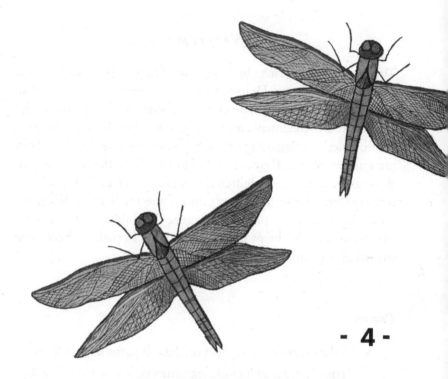

- **4** -

THE MONSTERS THAT SCARE US

We all have monsters that scare us. Mindfulness offers us concrete tools to be with those monsters, welcoming them rather than fleeing from them or pushing them away. This is contrary to our normal way of being. We generally do not like change and will do anything to hang on to the familiar. This adds to our suffering. Mindfulness helps us to realize we can be with our monsters in a different relationship. This liberates us and helps us to suffer less. When we see clearly, we are less likely to be hijacked by our thoughts and emotions. This allows us to be with, in an open and curious way, rather than run from with fear and trepidation. This requires bravery.

Warriors

There is something rich about a group of human beings who come together to meditate. Despite winter ice storm conditions and an influx of appointment cancelations, there are five persons who have braved the elements and are, sitting patiently in the waiting room, quietly anticipating our mindfulness meditation class. They are warriors to me. They are able to bravely be with self, even with those aspects that may frighten them. We can strengthen our inner bravery through the practice of mindfulness meditation. When we go to the breath, we come to recognize the fluidity of those scary situations, and this helps us to be with what is, without becoming overwhelmed and immobilized.

Practice

» Take a moment to reflect on default patterns that limit you. These may include fear, anxiety, low self-confidence, and previous unpleasant events.
» Be a warrior and brave the elements.
» The breath will anchor you if this is too overwhelmimg.

Man in black

It was 6:30 a.m.. I ran head down, cautious of uneven frozen crevices of ice. The flash of headlights lit my path. I looked up in the nick of time to dodge a darkly-dressed runner heading straight for me. Black hoodie, obscure sweatpants, darting pace, dichotomous smile. My music was loud, so his sudden appearance startled me.

Was this encounter a simple coincidence or a symbolic event

– meeting face-to-face with a bearer of pain – an unwelcome guest of darkness? We face this man in black daily. He creeps up on us with emotional vulnerability. He beats down our doors at times with demands and rawness.

Practice

>> Face this guest head on in your travels today.
>> Smile

Moving beyond those cocoons

As I was on my morning run, I came across three large holes burled into a snow bank. I remembered days gone by, when I was a child and played in the snow for hours, building what we referred to as snow forts. We spent many hours being in these crevices where we basked in silence, isolated from the outside world, cocooned from everyday life. It is easy to want to stay in this place of shelter. A cocoon of ignorance. A cocoon of distraction. A cocoon of non-reality. But the easiest path is not always the most beneficial. It takes courage to leave the cocoon, drop all of our preconceived notions and to allow ourselves to be as we are with all that we must endure. This new-found equanimity allows us to move beyond those cocoons and embrace the world.

Practice

>> Pause and go to the breath.
>> Reflect. Is there something or someone in your life that you would like to avoid?

» Ask yourself... "is this resistance contributing to my suffering?"
» Move forward, out of the cocoon that has sheltered you.
» Be free.

Facing Unpleasantness

Mindfulness helps one to be in the moment, even if the moment is unpleasant. It's accepting what is without trying to change it. It has not been a good week. There has been much unpleasantness. As I shut out the lights and crawled into bed, you can imagine my angst when I heard...drip...drip...drip. In my efforts to not be with what is, I justified that the noise must simply be the faucet dripping. I made my way down the stairs, in the dark, to the kitchen sink. No drip noise coming from there. Then I tried to convince myself that perhaps it was the ticking of the clock. It wasn't. Eventually, like a game of I Spy, I discovered that the roof was leaking. I located the source, only to realize this was the result of an ice dam, backed up under the shingles with the extreme winter temperature fluctuations. I wanted to just go back to bed, but instead, I paused, and with a new lens, realized I could deal with this inconvenience. I immediately called in a roofing company, who removed the snow and stopped the leak. Unpleasantness requires gently sitting with it when the dams emerge.

Practice

» When you wake up tomorrow morning take a moment to arrive before you do anything else.
» Breathe. Notice what's happening in the body, breath and

heart.

» Is there unpleasantness? Where do you feel it in your body?

» Do you want to shut your eyes and go back to sleep?

» Are there maladaptive coping mechanisms that you have adapted as a response to stress? ...Denial, numbing, shopping, drinking, busyness?

» Drop the judgment. Understand that it is human to want to escape when faced with unpleasantness.

» Be gentle with self. Proceed with curiosity and trust.

The race

My first glimpse of mindfulness awareness occurred during my first full marathon race. Many of you may have heard of the term "runners high." As I ran past the halfway point of the 42.6 kilometer course, I became profoundly aware of my running counterparts, my body seemingly moving in slow motion, and the cheers from encouraging spectators. They offered me hope and heartfelt best wishes. They echoed words like "you're almost there, hang on... it's all downhill from here." They looked at me with full presence. This allowed me to truly, for the first time, be completely in the moment.

It was with great sadness that I heard of the tragedy at the 2015 Boston Marathon. I have crossed the finish line thirteen times, exhausted and raw as waves of emotion have come over me. As a marathon runner, I felt deep compassion for all.

Practice

» Take five quiet minutes today to think about the importance of being a mindful society.

» The simple act of going to silence has the power to change everything

Get prepared to face your locomotives head on

I was travelling on business, visiting a small neighbouring community. This particular community is lovely with the exception of a raised train track overhead that allows for locomotives to barrel through the town at high speeds. Upon arrival, the bed and breakfast owner showed me to my room on the third story of a stately heritage home. I looked out the window, mystified by the vantage point of the overhead train track directly in front of me. I marveled at the thought of reaching out and almost touching it while daydreaming about the interactions of my day. At the end of the day, I settled in, turned the lights off, and went to bed.

I had no sooner fallen asleep when I was awakened by the sensation of the bed moving, the bellowing sound of engines, bright lights piercing through my window directly into my eyes. I was convinced that the train was coming through the room. My room's hue changed from dark and peaceful to bright and interrogating. This went on all night, on the hour. I had no choice but to literally look at these mighty locomotives in the eye each time they came barreling towards me. I had to accept what I could not change.

The practice of mindfulness helps us to face our challenges head on and when we do this, we too regain a sense of control and freedom. We can look at our locomotives in the eye, through the gift of equanimity or we can run. If we look at our challenges with curiosity and acceptance then they, in essence, become less threatening and less painful.

Practice

» Reach out...touch it...and let go.

Moving furniture

So much of our life is stationary and defined. One evening, just before bed, my wife made me aware of a watermark on our bedroom carpet. I automatically went into denial not wanting to admit that this might be a water leak. This is one of my biggest fears and I have had recurring dreams of water dripping into our home. With a flashlight in hand, I crawled up into the attic, looking for water damage, and found nothing. We looked beneath the room to find that water was dripping into our garage ceiling. Insurers were called, restoration units deployed and the cause of the problem traced to a broken water pipe. The entirety of a month was one of instability and sleeping on twin beds in the basement. Like spring that follows a long winter, we finally saw progress emerging. This inconvenience required the movement of furniture, necessary for the installation of new flooring, patchwork, and renewal. Moving furniture allowed for the emergence of new finds and the rediscovery of old treasures. The practice of mindfulness allows us to look at inconveniences in a different way, and appreciate new discoveries.

Practice

» Remember a time when something difficult revealed a silver lining.

Storm chasers

As we sat around the dinner table with Brown Eyes' boyfriend, he told us a story about his uncle being a storm chaser. With much excitement, he described his uncle's unique occupation. He identified that the job entailed extensive driving in a truck with all kinds of apparatus, searching for storms. I have always been fascinated by this concept.

I love to sit in a place of safety and watch a storm. Storms either find us or we find them. They touch us with turbulence and fury. The practice of mindfulness may catapult us into a profound presence to be with the pleasant, unpleasant and neutrality of life. We can be both participant and observer. This unique vantage point allows us to witness events as a quiet observer and this helps us to act more wisely when faced with disturbances.

Practice

- » Storms in our life come and go.
- » We have the apparatus to survive through them and potentially thrive as a result of them.
- » Take a moment to go to stillness and reflect with gentleness on the storms that you have weathered.

Jump

Why do we become comfortable with status quo? Many of us advocate for change in an effort to help others but neglect to advocate for self. This hesitation may be associated with our desire for predictability and our lack of comfort with upheaval. This fear of change hinders us from moving forward. This stagnation keeps us awake at night, rattles our confidence, and may challenge ethics. As "fixers," we shun away from fear of being labeled as a troublemaker, but the absence of action is an even worse consequence.

When we meditate, we become radically aware of habits and behaviours that may have served us until now. Once we recognize these, we come to realize that we can change.

Practice

» Take a few moments to reflect on a situation where you feel stuck.
» Pause and consider, in this moment, that you have choice.
» When ready, move forward with gentleness, confidence and jump.

Wake up...wake up...wake up!

Boo boom!!!!! In the wee hours of the morning, there was a loud crashing sound. I jumped up out of bed only to realize that this sound was thunder. My two young adult daughters, Brown Eyes and Blue Eyes, came bellowing into our bedroom, screaming "Dad... we're scared." I was amused by their regression to childhood, but I also secretly welcomed it.

Thunder storms have the potential to wake you up when they visit at night. They startle and remind you of powers much bigger. They reacquaint you with your own vulnerability. Mindfulness exposes all that we have constructed to protect us. Many of us don't like change. We cling to what we know and we attempt to push away the stormy circumstances of living. By going to silence we come to recognize that mindfulness can be the rainbow that fills the clear blue sky after a storm or that rich sunlight breaking through the dark clouds and warms you.

Practice

- » The next time there is a rain storm, find a place of safety, close your eyes, and just listen.
- » Notice the crescendo of the storm, its arrival, and departure.
- » Time the space between the cracks of thunder.
- » Use all of your senses.
- » Smell the scent of the air and notice if it changes through the storm's trajectory.
- » Feel the breeze on your skin. Feel the emotion that the storm wakes up.
- » If you feel overwhelmed or frightened at any time, focus on the breath to help ground you.

Acknowledge Loss

"Dad, is it better to acknowledge a loss or simply not talk about it?" asked my youngest, Brown Eyes. "Yes, you should definitely express your condolences rather than ignore loss," I responded. I then shared a story about an occurrence that immediately followed my father's death many years ago. There was a friend with whom I spent much time. I joined him for dinner. He spoke about everything but the passing of my father. He made no inquiries as to how I was coping. I was shocked at his omission, but more importantly, I was hurt.

Today is September 11th. The day continues to conjure up strong emotions. At the time of the World Trade Center's tragedy, I gathered newspapers, placed them into a bag, and put them into storage thinking that one day they might be historical or of interest to my two young daughters. Years later, they remain buried in the storage room, untouched. It hurts too much to look at them. It hurts too much to talk about it. But not acknowledging this traumatic event would be more wrong than right. So, to you, my dear friends, I need to say "I am so sorry for your loss...how are you managing?"

Practice

» If you know someone who is experiencing a loss, acknowledge it.
» Don't interrupt, offer advice or attempt to solve or fix.
» Just be with what's there, with full presence, mindfully.

I thought myself out of thoughts

I did so much thinking today that I thought myself out of thoughts. With my feet up, in front of one of my favourite television series, this line emerged. I thought about it – no pun intended. I let it permeate in my mind's memory compartment, hoping that my amygdala, hippocampus, cerebellum, and prefrontal cortex would help me to remember it. For safe measure, I jotted it down on a piece of paper. To me, it depicted so nicely what I often refer to it as the "monkey mind." This is the churning of excessive thoughts that ruminates in our consciousness, and at times, takes over our life. Unfortunately, thoughts do not always dissipate. They often multiply into big scary monsters that frighten and make us feel out of control. The practice of mindfulness helps to be with what's there. It helps us to pause, to realize that these thoughts are just thoughts and we are able to be at peace, even for a short time.

"What if's," "should haves," and "might have beens" fall to the wayside. Mindfulness gives us control and this can be life changing.

Practice

» When you find that your mind is spiraling, take some time to simply notice where your mind wanders.
» You may wish to label your thoughts into categories or words, like pain, fear, planning, regret, happiness etc.
» This mindfulness exercise helps you to observe your habitual thought patterns and recognize that some of these may not serve you.

Intention, Attention and Attitude

It scampered up the wall and maneuvered like Houdini through a tiny crack in the brick to a new and better land. In that instance, I realized that we had mice. Denial was no longer my ally to unprecedented sounds in the attic. I could no longer tell Brown Eyes that she was simply hearing things. I had to orchestrate a well-crafted plan to deal with these unwelcome intruders and it had to be prompt. Today, the pest control is coming to batten down the hatches. My garage has been emptied and the house prepared for action. At times, our lives are turned inside out by unwelcomed intruders. The practice of mindfulness is not magical, but it can provide us with the tools of confidence and awareness so that we can do more than just squeak through difficult situations. Mindfulness requires three key elements: Intention, Attention and Attitude. Intention involves knowing why we are doing what we are doing, when we are doing it. It is our vision. Attention involves attending fully to the present moment without preoccupation with the past or future. Attitude or how we pay attention, helps us to stay open, kind, and curious. These elements are foundational to our mindfulness practice.

Practice

» Bring to mind a current situation that is distressing.
» Remind yourself in the moment you are safe.
» Are you able, with full intention, to be present with this?
» Can you bring your full attention to this?
» Is your attitude able to be one of openness, curiosity, and kindness?

Unwelcome guests

A patient appealed to me that his father told him if he were good, then life would be good. At the time, I had no well-crafted reply. I wanted to tell him that things would get better with the passage of time, but I didn't want to sound dismissive. Part of me wanted to elaborate, that things sometimes happen for a reason, but in the depth of rawness, these words almost seem disrespectful, and the reason too distant to see. Sometimes, events simply do not make sense. They have no rhyme or reason. We can pray, bargain, and wish them away but they may linger like unwelcomed guests. They immobilize us. We can choose to push them away or greet them at the door.

Practice

» Take a moment to be with it all...that which is pleasant and unpleasant, without judgment and interruption.

The meeting

We had the opportunity to meet the parents of the young man who is dating our eldest daughter, Blue Eyes. We quite like this fellow. He is caring, hardworking, and kind. It seems like it was only yesterday I was meeting my Wise Wife's parents and amused how history is repeating itself.

Meeting the parents is both exciting and unnerving. You want what is best for your children. You want it to go smoothly for them. Mindfulness requires that we meet ourselves in this moment, as if for the very first time. This can be uncomfortable. We might see things we like. There may be patterns or behaviours we do not like. This journey can be both exciting and unnerving. By the way...we loved the parents!

Practice

> »   Meet yourself as you are right now in this moment.
> »   Notice the breath. Is it rapid or slow?
> »   What's happening in the weather of the mind?
> »   What emotions are conjured?
> »   Trust that you can be with all of this.
> »   If at any time you are overwhelmed, you may ground yourself by bringing attention to the in breath and the out breath.

Begin again

What was this change in my body? I pride myself on being in touch with this living, breathing organism. I do mindfulness meditation daily; I run, cycle and I try to nurture my creative soul. Yet, I found myself shuffling from one doctor to another. What I had chalked up to be a simple nasal infection was soon being investigated to rule out something more sinister.

Yesterday, I entered our local hospital, went through the motions of new patient registration, had my photograph taken, weighed in, and waited for an assessment and a potentially life changing diagnosis. I did all of the typical things that one might do in these circumstances. I bartered, I planned what I needed to accomplish, I reminisced, I prayed, I cried, and I became angry. I questioned "Why me and not them?" I sat for three hours, waiting to see a specialist, and then I was directed into an examination room.

I spouted off my medical history, my symptomatology, and my fears in record time. The physician pulled his chair close to me, listening attentively and kindly, and then examined me. He was calming, compassionate, and I understood he was a survivor himself. He knew my fear. In that moment, he and I were separate yet connected. He advised that this was not a serious diagnosis. I sat numb, relieved and grateful.

Yesterday, I was fearful. Today, the world seems new and extraordinary. The things I thought were monumental are unimportant as I savour each and every moment as if for the first time. I woke up humming. When I ran, I opened my eyes to the shimmering sunshine on the lake. I observed the silhouettes of the trees and played tag with my shadow.

Practice

» The next time you are presented with a scary monster, greet it with eyes wide open.
» Stand firm in the knowledge that your breath will ground you and provide stability.
» Allow it to be your teacher.

Re-forgetting

The lyrics "I go out just so I can re-forget" echoed from my earbuds as I walked to work. So many of us try to escape suffering through distraction. Perhaps re-forgetting fortifies the fight required to keep on going. But re-forgetting only contributes to more distress. What about re-constructing? Let's utilize mindfulness tools that will assist us in facing challenges with full confidence.

Practice

» Are there situations that you choose to forget?

» The invitation is to invite those occurrences with kindness and gentleness.

» Notice how maladaptive coping tendencies (numbing, distracting, avoiding, over-indulging) distract rather than assist.

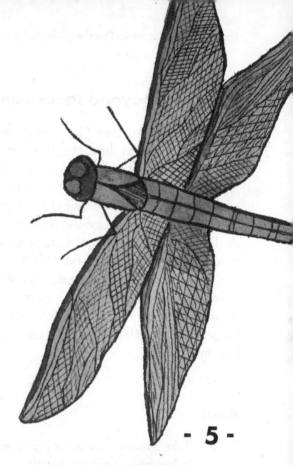

- 5 -

MISPERCEPTIONS

How often have you judged someone or something and been wrong? When we categorize people, we fail to acknowledge their uniqueness, their beauty, and their basic goodness. This usually happens when we are immersed in our own self-doubt. When we feel threatened, we will do anything to protect ourselves, sometimes even at the expense of others. All beings in this world want to be loved. Ignorance separates us and builds walls. Fear blinds us, limits our capacity to think, and diminishes our ability to see what is really there. This contributes to rigidity and tunnel vision. No person benefits from either.

Beyond square and rigid

Brrrrrr! Minus 40 degrees Celsius with the wind chill. I bundled up and went out to start the car to give it extra time to warm up before leaving for work. The frigid weather reminded me of twenty-five years ago, when I hopped into the car on what was the coldest day of the year for the birth of our eldest daughter, Blue Eyes, the tires so frozen they were square and rigid. It was only when I arrived at the hospital that they softened and became more pliable. We can be rigid in our view of the world. Mindfulness equips us with a new lens from which to observe situations both externally and internally in real time. This assists us to be more emotionally intelligent with decision making, devoid of preconceived reactions that may no longer serve us. Mindfulness helps our minds to be more pliable... less rigid.

Practice

» Take 5 minutes to bring your attention to the breath – the in-breath and the out-breath.
» This practice is an invitation to notice if anything softens.

Labels

She spoke with clarity and candour. She had been labeled with a mental health diagnosis that she did not understand or like. She questioned its appropriateness and she felt misdiagnosed. She articulated that she had none of those symptoms, the ones that are synonymous with "being crazy" rather than different or eccentric.

Labels hurt. We use them to identify and they often take away dignity. We know these labels well...the non-compliant, the personality disorder, the trouble maker, the whiner, the squeaky wheel. When we drop our one-upmanship through the practice of mindfulness we allow for non-judgment, curiosity, and compassion. We group people through appreciation of connection rather than stigma and misperception.

Practice

>> Bring to mind a person whom you have labelled.
>> Did you form judgements based on preconceived ideas, beliefs or past experiences?
>> Can you look at that person with beginner eyes in a new way?

CPR for the soul

We were sitting around the table with Brown Eyes and her boyfriend. Somehow, we got onto the topic of mindfulness meditation and the classes that we were teaching. I was putting out feelers to see if these two might be interested. I spoke about it being like "CPR for the soul." Then, to our surprise, the boyfriend enthusiastically said "Yes, I would be very interested...I would definitely like to take this course." I was pleased to be able to offer the gift of mindfulness, and hoped it might be helpful for the rest of his life. He continued "Yes, I would really like to take CPR." Not quite what I had interpreted but not so bad! Sometimes, our clients, colleagues and superiors take what we say out of context. Their responses might be out of sync with our intentions, although heartfelt. We can look at the situation with curiosity and even with humour at times.

Practice

» Bring to mind a communication that was misinterpreted.
» What role did you both play in this?
» What would you do differently the next time?
» How can the practice of mindfulness help?

"You lift people's spirits and soul's every day."

We went shopping yesterday with a mission to purchase new outdoor chairs. We combed the aisles and then we laid our eyes on four beautiful cherry-red Adirondack chairs. I tried one out and my Wise Wife followed suit, both of us anticipating the hours of tranquility that these chairs would bring. As I attempted to place them onto a large shopping trolley, one of the employees quickly leapt to assist me.

When driving home I reflected that the fellow who assisted me looked older than me. I let my masculine pride get the better of me, incensed that he felt the need to come to my rescue in lifting the chairs. I doubted my abilities until my Wise Wife responded "He is used to lifting heavy things but you lift people's spirits and souls every day."

So often we feel undervalued and unappreciated. Often this is what we perceive rather than what is reality. It is important that we recognize the significant contributions that we make every day.

Practice

» Today, take a few moments to sit quietly.

» Allow the breath to ground you.
» Bring to mind how you too lift people's spirits and souls daily.
» Notice where you feel this in your body.

Speculation

Mindfulness helps us to pay attention to the body and how stress physically impacts us so that we can observe with clarity, pause, and then respond. I just received an email. My amygdala is catapulted into full action. I begin to feel my heart rate increasing, some nervousness, and respiration imbalance. My stomach churns. I habitually go to my catastrophizing mode, inviting currents of negativity to overwhelm me. I am thrown into speculation. But what if I'm wrong? What if this email is simply an inquiry? What if it's coming from a good heart? I have had some space. Now I will respond.

Practice

» You do not have to respond immediately to emails or text messages.
» It is empowering and wise to form a response, and then let it be.
» Return to it after giving yourself some space.
» If still sits right with you, then send it.

Make every moment count

My eldest daughter, Blue Eyes, has taken it upon herself to cleanse and heal after a challenging spring. She is exhausting my Wise Wife and me in the process, seeking day trips, hot yoga, spin classes, walking to work and a twelve-kilometre rugged hiking trail referred to as the "Cup and Saucer." This trail is dotted with countless stairs, steep inclines and jagged cliffs.

When we arrived at the trail my daughter announced that this was to be completed in a manner that would get her heart rate up. This was her way of saying that this was not going to be a leisurely hike. We persevered. We climbed, jumped over logs, and ducked under branches. We chatted about life and marveled at the beauty that surrounded us. What I had anticipated to be onerous and difficult was in fact unexpectedly delightful. An opportunity to see differently and to make every moment count.

Practice

> » Take some time this week to explore a new experience.
> » Use all of your senses to experience the moment.

Daisies and Devil's Paintbrushes

Such a dichotomy! Conversely, the white and yellow wispy petals of the daisy that determine if one loves you or loves you not. On the other hand, the constricted fiery orange blossoms of a flower considered a troublesome weed. The finishing line of my daily run puts me in a field filled with both plants for as far as the eye can see. But why must we label one as desirable and the other as undesirable? Why do we allow ourselves to get caught up in judgment and preconceived notions?

One of the seven tenants of mindfulness is to abandon fixed mindsets and be open to whatever arrives with curiosity and non-judgment, welcoming all.

Practice

> » Notice the beauty in both the flowers and the weeds.

The Whistler

As I was getting ready for bed, I heard it again – The Whistler. Coming from a home in my neighbourhood, I could hear the infectious sound of whistling.

This sound has intrigued me for the past year. I have heard it blend with the robins in the spring, during warm summer nights and the sound of crickets, and now with the rustling of autumn leaves. There have been times when I have stepped out the front door in my quest to discover the whistler's identity, determined to solve this mystery. Yet there it was again, still unknown and still giving me solace at the end of my day. I have a preconceived notion that none of my neighbours could possibly be The Whistler.

We label and form judgments. Mindfulness facilitates clarity and full presence. It allows us to hear The Whistler and to be delighted when we come to know his identity.

Practice

> » Take a moment to whistle with awareness.
> » Allow your lips to pucker and whistle with the inhalation.

» Notice how this sounds and feels.
» Then purse your lips and whistle with the exhalation.
» Is the sound the same?
» How has it changed, if at all, from the inhalation?
» Mindful whistling is a nice auditory way of appreciating the in breath and the out breath.

What is real and what is not

As I approached my car parked in a dusk-lit parking lot, my eye caught the sight of a young man on a skateboard who sailed by me. His shirt was enblazened with Thrasher in bold letters. My associations with the word were not favourable. I took a purposeful pause, tuned into my body, and noticed how my fight or flight response triggered instinctively. I got in the car and felt a sense of relief as the door automatically locked. He swept back and forth on his skateboard like a pendulum in front of me. My pulse quickened. My breath became shallow. Time slowed. My mind spiraled. In the end there was nothing to be concerned about. In fact, I am not even sure he noticed me. My mind simply jumped ahead, causing me anguish. Mindfulness helps us to recognize this spiral and know we have choice. I was wrong.

Practice

» Bring to mind a time when your mind spiraled.
» How did this spiraling affect you?
» Did your worries materialize?
» Is there something to be learned?
» Now take a moment to breathe and feel grounded.

Smile

I am amazed at the connection that a simple smile can bring. During my daily running and walking excursions, I delight in this opportunity. When I least expect it, a passerby gives me an unexpected smile. I experience an immediate connection and it feels good. When I worked at the hospital there was a staff member who would seldom look up upon passing. I quickly formed judgment. I disliked walking by them, and after a while, I stopped smiling or trying to engage. Sadly, I felt justified with my behaviour. In hindsight, I did not know the suffering that this person was experiencing. I had misperceived. As human beings, we all suffer.

Practice

» Take time to connect with others today, and if you can, smile.
» Notice what happens in your body, thoughts, and emotions.

The hunch

Last evening, it happened. After many weeks of speculation, our suspicions were confirmed. My daughter, Blue Eyes, has been updating her social media pages and a young man has been appearing with increased frequency. Photographs have changed from selfies to couples and my Wise Wife says our daughter seems to be quite "smitten" with this fellow. He offers her presence and connection, and she seems to be thriving in his good company. This is more than just a hunch. When we are mindful, we are more in touch with our inner wisdom.

Practice

- » Pay attention to your hunches.
- » Notice where they emerge from within.
- » Allow these insights to help you to see clearly.
- » Be responsive.

Accepting imperfection

When the season of Christmas comes around, I often immerse myself in rich tradition and ritual. Self-expectations in our workplaces and in our personal lives are high. We become exhausted. This revelation occurred to me as I lugged an eight-foot balsam spruce tree into the house. I struggled to keep it afloat, pulled it through a narrow door frame, and stepped on evergreen needles that trailed behind me. This exercise reaffirmed that this would be the last real Christmas tree for us. It just seemed like far too much work getting it to stand upright, watering it, and decorating it. It had to be perfect in my eyes and anything less than this was not acceptable.

Ironically, it was only when I "let go" of the preconceived expectations to truly savour the moment that I could truly enjoy the experience. Letting go offered me an opportunity to relinquish my self-imposed expectations. It invited me to realize that the tree did not have to be perfect.

Practice

- » The next time that you are feeling overwhelmed, stop for a moment and check in.

» Ask yourself the following questions. Must this be perfect? Am I making this more difficult than it has to be?
» Breathe. Use all of your senses to sit with what emerges.
» Sit with what truly is.

A framework for communication

There are often significant communication challenges in the workplace. This can contribute to a lack of trust, poor communication, misperceptions, and low staff morale. Yesterday, four stories of scaffolding began to appear outside of my office window. Wood and steel fortresses seamlessly erected by a team of young men. As I worked at my desk, I could hear their conversations through my open window. Initially, I was annoyed with the multitude of obscenities and level of noise, but then I became more curious. I found myself listening attentively and even laughing at their banter. They called each other names, cursed with every sentence, and laughed furiously. They spoke with excitement about their families, their favourite things to do, and their plans for the weekend. There were no side conversations, no passive aggressiveness, no placating, no playing the victim. Communication was to the point. Crystal clear. There was no holding back. They clearly stated what was on their minds without judgment or intimidation.

Practice

» Let the scaffolding between your heart and your brain provide you with a solid structure from which to respond.

Worn

A pair of men's leather shoes lay discarded on a pile of dirty snow. Those shoes have a story to tell. They may have supported the person who wore them; they may have been worn with confidence and conviction by a business executive striving for success in a boardroom; they may have danced at a wedding; they may have been a gift from a loved one. At one time, they were shiny and new. Like these shoes, we all have a story to tell. Exterior appearances might be worn and tattered; however, there is a basic goodness in all of us, just waiting to be nurtured and awakened.

Practice

> » Bring intentional awareness to those you meet today.
> » Open your eyes to see beneath the surface.
> » Notice their storyline.
> » Discard judgment.
> » Are you able to witness their basic goodness?

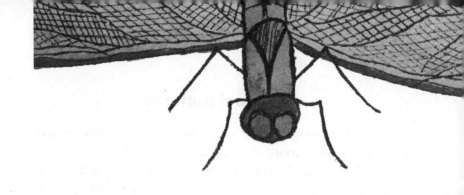

YOUR OWN VULNERABILITY

Stress is often understood to be that which we perceive is beyond our physical, emotional, and spiritual resources to manage. When we are confronted by stressful situations, we may fight, flee or become immobilized. We feel vulnerable, naked, and exposed. Mindfulness can be instrumental in helping us to be patient, allow things to unfold in their own accord, act wisely, and know this will pass. Mindfulness allows us to recognize the habitual patterns and behaviours that become our default mode. This awareness helps us to decipher if and how this serves us. This is the first tangible step to making change. When we pause and go to the breath, we wake up our capacity to self-regulate and proceed with emotional intelligence.

Habitual patterns

I am always fascinated by the forgiving nature of the human body. In times of celebration, we may consume excessive amounts of sugar, calories, and alcohol. We may attempt to get back on track with healthy diet and more regular exercise. This lasts until the next celebratory occasion when we fall back into this pattern – eating too much, living with remorse, and further good intentions. Although the body tends to be resilient, bouncing back becomes more difficult with each incident. Over time this pattern leaves an unkind footprint on the body. The mind/body relationship is inseparable and the cycle goes on. We see this in ourselves. We witness this in those we love. Once we are able to understand this pattern, we are able to gently and firmly get back on track with self-compassion rather than self-criticism. Mindfulness helps us to realize these habitual patterns and know that we have choice.

Practice

» Breathe.
» Consider exceptional events that you experienced this week (pleasant or unpleasant).
» Acknowledge your habitual behavioral patterns, thoughts, and emotions.
» Are these conditioned reactions?
» Remember, you have a choice.

Home

After a lovely two-week visit, we ceremoniously brought our daughter, Brown Eyes, to the airport. We said our goodbyes, made sure that we could see her on the other side of the glass windows through security, and waved goodbye. I felt grateful, sad, and proud. We had left the airport and were driving down the road when she called to tell us her flight was canceled. We immediately turned around and my Wise Wife went into the airport to offer her support and guidance. Another goodbye.

One hour later, we received news that the flight was going to be further delayed. This occurred hour after hour. Finally, nine hours later, we received a text that she was in the plane, on the tarmac, and ready to depart. We breathed a sigh of relief. Half an hour later, she called in tears asking to be picked up as the flight was, again, cancelled. She was worn-out, hungry, and discouraged. She felt helpless and that her situation was out of control. She just wanted to get home.

Our lives are frequently interrupted by cancellations and delays. When we are experiencing upheaval, we just want to arrive home safely. Home is the place that brings us solace and shelter when we feel vulnerable. Mindfulness helps us to realize we can be at home wherever we are, with all that we face, as a silent observer, safe. We come to realize, whatever troubles we are experiencing, we have the inner resources and capacity to be with it, knowing it will pass.

Practice

> »   There is power and pleasure in being present.
>
> »   Remind yourself, when you feel helpless, that you really do have power.
>
> »   You can find home in whatever unpleasantness you face.

The path

Yesterday, I made my way to our pharmacy to pick up a prescription. I announced my name, expecting the script would be ready since I had dropped it off the previous day. I was met with an apology that it was not ready, and an invitation to sit and wait. I did so. This offered me an opportunity to be still and observe others as they interacted with the busy clerk separated by a thin slice of counter. Many were impatient. Many were demanding and specifying how, when, who, and why they needed their medications in a certain fashion. Some raised their voices. Some wept with frustration. Some threatened to call their insurer or take their business elsewhere. Some approached in wheelchairs. Some approached upright. As a quiet observer, this experience reinforced the concept that we all suffer in some capacity. It is part of our human condition. Rather than being with our suffering, we wish for relief – a quick fix. This sometimes comes at the expense of others who come between us and our remedy. We all have a story to tell. Sometimes, it is filled with sheer delight. Sometimes, it is raw with anguish. The practice of mindfulness helps us to be with all of this, but even more important, it helps us to be kind to each other along the path.

Practice

» Find yourself in a busy place.
» Breathe, and connect with your body, thoughts and emotions.
» Drop judgment.
» Be a quiet observer. Just be.

Acceptance

The needle was inserted to freeze my gums and I waited with trepidation for the dentist to return while the anesthetic took effect. I ask myself, how is it that I got here again, as I glance at the tray of sterile instruments waiting patiently to befriend my mouth. I robotically proceed through the motions – mouth wide open, metal clamps affixed, drills grinding, chatter in the backdrop. A radio spewing out seventies rock music. A modification of the body. An acceptance of what is. There is freedom in accepting the pleasant and unpleasant of life.

Practice

- » When you find yourself in a vulnerable situation, be present with it.
- » Breathe.
- » When your mind starts to wander, gently escort it back to the breath.
- » This allows for the switch from the sympathetic nervous system to the parasympathetic nervous system.
- » Doing so helps us to see more clearly.

Loss of Innocence

I settled into my chair amongst the backdrop of spring sounds and wondered what I would possibly write about. My day was filled with contradictions that challenged me ethically and made it very difficult to be supportive without judgment. Today, a new patient arrived to my office, and with head looking downward, began to tell me their story. I heard things I wished I never had to hear. I felt torn as feelings of disgust settled in my gut and a sense of empathy as I listened. I longed for the ignorance I once had as a young man just entering the profession. Years of exposure to constant and profound descriptions of pain have weathered my psyche and part of me wanted to say "enough!" So, together, we sat in the pain. We explored it with curiosity and I laid it to rest with this writing.

Practice

> » Prepare to write mindfully with full awareness.
> » Set yourself up in a comfortable place with a timer, notebook and pen.
> » Breathe. Cultivating gentleness and kindness to self.
> » Bring to mind something that is unsettling.
> » Set the timer for ten minutes.
> » Allow for authenticity and vulnerability.
> » Free write without stopping, beginning with the sentence... "In this moment"...
> » Just keep writing until there is nothing left to be said or the alarm rings.
> » Then read what you have written out loud to self.
> » Be open to insights without judgment.
> » Notice how you feel now compared to how you felt at the beginning of this practice.

Side-swiped

Driving 100 kilometers an hour in the far-left lane of a multi-lane highway, I noticed a large truck edging its way over. Initially, I thought, surely, he must see me. However, the driver continued to come into my lane which forced me to swerve left in an effort to miss being hit. Within minutes, we were side-swiped. We felt a sudden tug as two sheets of metal collided against each other. Friction and a close brush.

Sometimes, we need to experience fear to remind us how lucky we are to be alive. We are fine, no injuries, lots of scrapes to the car. A nudge to wake up now.

Practice

» Breathe.
» Then bring to mind a situation in your life when you may have had a near miss.
» Did you learn from this event?
» How has it shown up in your life, if at all?
» Have you slipped back into old habits that may not serve you well?
» What obstacles hinder you from living your life differently?
» Are you willing to commit to change?
» How will you bring mindfulness into your daily life at this time?

The bath

There is something so soothing about the experience of a warm bath. It encapsulates you and stills you in the moment. It invites you in and contains you with your nakedness and vulnerability. It accepts your authentic self without judgment. It shelters you from the busyness of everyday life and offers you comfort.

Many years ago, I had the misfortune of being hospitalized for a lengthy period of time. I found myself feeling trapped in a building with windows that did not open to the outside world. I was in much pain and I could not do much except lay in the hospital bed that had become my nemesis. I felt alienated. I longed to feel human again. Part of the re-humanization process entailed a visit from an older French-Canadian nun and nurse, who would arrive at my room each evening and ask if I would like to be bathed. Initially, I felt uncomfortable with this idea, but as time passed, I welcomed this gentle guest. As she sponge bathed me, I felt deep appreciation during this time of helplessness.

Practice

» Like a warm bath, mindfulness can provide us with an opportunity for time out.

» Allow mindfulness to embrace all that is

» Allow it to bathe you and be part of your re-humanizing process.

» Treat yourself to a warm bath.

» Lock the door and "be."

Colour, beauty, hope

Each summer, I shop to find the right patio lanterns. I usually buy, hang up, return, and buy again until I get the right fit, the right hue and the right ambience. Then, like a child with beginner's eyes, I wait for the sun to set and look out the window with delight, anticipating this light in the darkness.

We all have challenging or difficult times in life. The patio lanterns, in some way, represent a beacon of light and hope. They light a pathway to a new way of being when we feel defeated. They offer colour, beauty and hope. The practice of mindfulness has the potential to illuminate pathways in our lives that we may not be aware. Many of our pathways, we travel by default. Shedding light and colour on these habits can help us to see the world with more luminosity.

Practice

> » Bring to mind a time when a beacon of light has illuminated your path.
> » This could have been in the form of a person, a kind word, an unexpected gift, a pleasant surprise, or even a kind gesture to self.
> » Enjoy this memory with clarity, hope and self-compassion.
> » Find the beauty in all of it.

Equanimity

Waiting in a physiotherapy treatment room. We are all there to heal our injuries. Four of us lined up on plinths. The television is placed strategically in front of us. It lulls us to sleep. No words are exchanged. We are all there to rid ourselves of pain. There are buzzer sounds that chime on and off as machines cycle around treatment needs. Every so often, there is an inquiry...how are you feeling? "Now we're going to do this. Now we're going to apply this and hook you up to that. This is going to be cold so get ready. This might hurt...etc."

My worries are insignificant. My injuries will heal. Mindfulness helps me to recognize the transient nature of my pain and this relieves my suffering.

Practice

» Take a seated position that you can sustain for ten minutes.
» Scan your body for any discomfort, tension, tightness, pain.
» Bring a focused awareness to this area without attempting to change it.
» Bring your awareness to the breath as it is in this moment.
» Notice its transient nature.

Naked

My hours of work have changed in order to make the best use of my new morning time. I drop my family off to their places of work and school, and head to the gym for an early morning cardio workout. It is my attempt to seize the moment and to feel healthy. After an hour of running and cycling, I hit the changeroom for the reward of a hot shower.

I sauntered into the shower area, donning a two-foot by four-foot gym-size paper-thin towel, eager to cleanse and get to work. As I walked around the corner, to my surprise, I met face to face with a female cleaning staff, rinsing down the showers like a fireman on a lifesaving mission. She pointed the giant hose in my direction and told me I could go ahead and shower while she continued to clean. She advised that she "had been in the business for years and had seen it all before!"

I quickly made my way behind the flimsy plastic shower curtain and took my shower, and so did the guy beside me and the guy beside him. I felt a bit sorry for the guy who came around the corner to shower and decided not to don a towel! Then it hit me. This was the perfect illustration of living in autopilot. This lady seemed oblivious to the naked men standing in the same small quarters, separated by laser-thin sheets of plastic. We too may be oblivious to what is right in front of us.

Practice

» With intention bring your awareness to something that is alive. It may be a plant, an animal, a tree, or a person.
» Look with new eyes.
» Drop judgment.
» Just notice.

I hate to admit it, but my wife was right!

Another year, another Christmas light fiasco! Each year, just after Halloween, the ghouls and goblins are removed from the store shelves, only to be replaced by Christmas paraphernalia. This usually signifies urgency at getting the car winter-worthy, the yard tidied, and the outdoor Christmas lights tested, connected, and up. We have been in our home for eighteen years, and that tiny three-foot greenhouse bargain blue spruce now stands tall and could challenge any evergreen tree in the forest. The dilemma, however, is that my wife still wants that backyard blue spruce to be decorated with fifteen sets of tiny incandescent red lights from treetop to trunk.

Saturday was the last calm before the storm and perhaps the last chance for putting up the outdoor Christmas lights without having to tread in waist-high snow. I thought I would take it upon myself to get the stepladder and attack that forty-foot tree in an effort to surprise my wife. I mounted the stepladder, grabbed a twelve-foot wooden pole, and began the process by threading the strand of lights like a tailor threads a needle and thread. I clung to that ladder, twisted and contorted, and dangled the pole upwards attempting to loop that one branch that would allow me to continue the process. A neighbour came around, checked to see if I was alright, and delivered a story about an acquaintance who attempted to hang lights alone and ended up hanging upside down with his foot snagged in the ladder's top rung. This did not settle me or help me to delight in the moment. I just wanted to get the lights up, get down, and get warm.

After an hour, I retreated and looked for another lighting alternative. Perhaps the lights would look best this year intertwined around the patio pergola, I thought. I sat, looking and alternating my sight between the blue spruce and the pergola, frustrated and feeling old. It was then my wife arrived home. She made it clear she did not wish to argue but there was no way the lights would be placed on the pergola, and in my heart of hearts, I knew she was right. Hence, I decided to have a good nap, a cup of tea, and a go at it the next day with my dear wife. Lights went on the second time like a charm, and with childlike excitement, I turned them on and stood back, gazing in awe. Upon reflecting, my wife reminded me that she was right. My retort was "you're not inaccurate with a lot of what you say." Talk about lack of clarity with that placating response! Her response was "of course not...it's my reality."

We are often so caught up in the task at hand that we neglect to be truly present. We may attempt to placate, but we fool no one with our habitual and automatic responses. Mindfulness awareness lights up our authenticity. I hate to say it, but my Wise Wife was right!

Practice

- » Breathe.
- » Recall a recent difficult communication with someone.
- » Take a moment to reflect.
- » Were you able to be fully present and truly listen?
- » Did you have your own agenda and preconceived notions?
- » Did you placate?
- » Would you do something different next time?

ALL THAT YOU EAT OR DRINK

So often we want a quick fix and we want it now. We consume copious amounts of calories and high processed fatty foods. We eat mindlessly, often in front of our devices, oblivious to what we are putting into our mouths. To make matters worse, we are no happier with this way of being. I was first introduced to mindful eating at a silent retreat many years ago. The task at hand was to eat using all of our senses, in silence without having eye contact with others. The latter was especially difficult given our cultural and societal expectations surrounding food. Food gathers us around the table. It conjures up emotion and sentiment. It is indeed something to be celebrated but we have turned it into just another thing to do. When we eat or drink mindfully, we enjoy what we consume more and we feel healthier, slowing down and actually eating less.

Pie in the sky

"There is a very good pie shop across the street" was all that our friend needed to say to us to influence our plans for the day in Toronto. The shop is called Wanda's Pie in the Sky and it seemed like the ideal place for two foodies to satisfy their gastronomic desires. My daughter, Blue Eyes, is getting married and my future son-in-law and I scanned an assortment of pies while the ladies were on the hunt for the right wedding dress. As I took that first bite of my British Columbian sour cherry pie and my young accomplice indulged in a piece of wild blueberry pie, we knew that we got the better deal. We quietly enjoyed every morsel, occasionally coming up for air to comment and to smile. We didn't have to say much. We just knew we were enjoying each other's company and Wanda's was about to become our go-to spot. The gift of true presence allows us to truly connect with one another and with all that we eat and drink. This is not a pie in the sky idea.

Practice

- » Eat one meal mindfully.
- » Go to silence.
- » Make sure there are no distractions.
- » Take one bite, using all of your senses.
- » Continue eating with full awareness.

A recipe for comfort

The weather has shifted once again, transitioning from freezing rain and fog to crisp, colder temperatures, and light snow. Walking home, I could feel the weather in my bones. I just wanted to arrive and get warm. When I entered the house, it greeted me with an aroma of homemade chicken soup. There was an array of textures and scents. Carrots, onions, celery, parsley all interwoven in a clear broth. My Wise Wife felt very good with her creation, content she had made something so appreciated from next to nothing. It was just a mixture of what she could find in the bottom of the refrigerator. A drawing upon inner resources. A recipe for comfort.

Practice

> » When looking in your pantry and refrigerator, pay attention to what is there.
> » The pickings may be sparse, and it may be time to shop for groceries; however, the invitation is to notice what is there, not what is missing.
> » Make a list of what you are grateful for.

Nectar of the Gods

Enjoying my morning coffee, before anyone awakened and even before the sun arose, I relished the silence. Taking in the warmth of the coffee as the mug rested in the palms of my hands, massaging them, waking up their circulation. The clock on the wall ticked rhythmically. I smiled as I recalled it was a ticking clock. I felt my heartbeat, and heard the sound of my breath. I savoured each drop of what my mother-in-law referred to as "nectar of the Gods."

As I sat and gazed out of the window, lights began to appear in the neighbouring houses, one by one. Others were awakening to another day.

Practice

» Set your alarm to awaken 15 minutes earlier tomorrow morning.
» Give yourself permission to slow down and enjoy a warm beverage.
» Breathe.
» Notice what is happening internally as well as externally.
» Savour.

Refresh

It's midafternoon and I am at my desk, sipping a cup of mint tea. It is the first opportunity in my busy day to pause. I drink it undistracted with full awareness. It warms my hands and I feel the temperature of the cup change as I hold it. The hot water envelops the tea bag and the smell intensifies with the passing moments. This is time just for me. No guilt. No lists to make. No tasks to get done. I don't want it to end. The tea that is fittingly called Refresh offers me time to just be.

Practice

» Take 15 minutes in your busy day to enjoy a cup of herbal tea, mindfully.

» Notice its texture, warmth, aroma, temperature, and colour.
» Hold it in your hand until you feel ready to take that first sip.
» Take one sip and use all of your sense to experience it with full awareness.
» Notice how the flavour changes as it steeps.
» Notice how its colour deepens.
» Notice as the temperature of the cup cools.
» Enjoy.

Half a dozen honey glazed donuts

While working from home this morning, I decided to hop in the car and drive to a nearby bakery renowned for its fine pastries.

I entered the premises and sized up the patrons, sipping freshly brewed coffee and nibbling on a host of tantalizing sweet delights. You see, I have a thing for bakeries. In fact, I often scout out bakeries when I visit new communities. One of my favourite reoccurring dreams entails me standing before a showcase of fresh-baked goods, strategizing which pastry I should select. So, you can imagine that when the baker told me this morning's honey glazed donuts would be ready in five minutes, that I would be inclined to wait.

This visit resulted in a return home with half-a-dozen warm honey glazed donuts, a loaf of rye and a package of cinnamon rolls. To my delight, I opened the bag, placed my fingers on one of the warm donuts, and put it to my mouth licking every drop of honey and enjoying the rich soft warm texture, tasting the sweetness like it was the first time. So often we miss the moment when we eat. Yet today, I ate mindfully and enjoyed each and every bite.

Practice

- » Take a few minutes to really savour the moment.
- » Grab a freshly brewed cup of coffee or a cup of your favourite tea, and a pastry and enjoy it mindfully.
- » Use all of your senses to truly be with your food.
- » Feast on what's present.
- » Bring your attention to its texture, smell, sound, and taste.
- » Think about its story and how it feels to allow it into your body.
- » Gently bring your awareness to every bite.
- » Delight in it.

A treat for an unpleasant day

While visiting our youngest daughter, Brown Eyes, now a teacher, she told us about a cupcake bakery she had learned about after a student's mother delivered twenty-two gourmet cupcakes to her classroom. We set out on a mission to find it. When we arrived, we quickly purchased eight unique cupcakes for afternoon tea. We devoured seven and one remained. I suggested that we freeze it so that Brown Eyes could enjoy it at the end of a challenging workday. In fact, I placed it in the freezer and labeled it "A treat for an unpleasant day."

We all have challenging work days. Some days are taxing and depleting. We all need a gift from time to time that will slow us down, bring us to the moment, and give us a sense of replenishment. Make sure to build this into your busy schedules. This is a vital requirement for sustainability and workplace wellness.

Practice

> » Can you reflect and bring to mind an activity that brings you great pleasure?
> » This may be an activity that you have not engaged in for quite some time.
> » Take some time to carve out space to enjoy this activity. This may be going for a walk, chatting with a friend, playing a musical instrument, or maybe reading a book.
> » Incorporate this into your day, week, or month on a regular basis.
> » Treat it as a vital requirement for wellness.

Candy

Everyday there is a pile of "to do" tasks. These are carried from day to day, and unless there is an imposed deadline, they continue to accumulate. My day starts off with the best of intentions. My plan is to get on top of my tasks, but by the day's end, many of these tasks become a never-ending pile of good intentions that is evidence of a repetitive and self-defeating pattern. We may have well-meaning intentions. We attempt to deal with the daily grind and we try to strategize ways to be more "on top of things" but we continue to be caught in competing demands in the workplace, in our personal lives and in the energy that we have. Consequently, we function in autopilot. On this day, autopilot for me was heading to the nearest confectionary to purchase a chocolate bar. My mindful intention was to search out a quiet place where I could meditate for 10 minutes. Yet my attention quickly diverted to a quick fix, which was a candy bar. This may have satisfied a craving in the short term. As part of the human condition, it is so easy to get diverted and caught in an autopilot reaction. When we stop and bring mindful awareness, we can make a conscious choice to intentionally attend to some self-care with mindfulness practice.

Practice

» Begin to pay attention to your stress triggers.
» Notice what happens in your mind, body and feelings during these events.
» With curiosity and non-judgment, explore your food intake as it relates to your stress levels.
» Understand that change can only occur with realization of habitual patterns.
» Be gentle with self.

Sandwiches and mindfulness

We have a six-foot, four-inch giant living with us for the summer. He is gangly, generally a happy fellow and is eating us out of house and home. We like to think that we are offering him a home and a loving family, and he in turn offers us many opportunities to learn from him.

Each evening, he takes out a loaf of bread and methodically conjures up three sandwiches in preparation for his lunch the next day. First, he puts Dijon mustard on the bread. Then he carves precisely three one by three-inch slices of cheddar on each. He then takes a red onion and slices it thinly and with precision, gently cutting it into wedges that he lays clockwise around the circumference of the bread. This is followed by three slices of genoa salami, a slice of turkey, and then crowned with baby spinach. He builds these sandwiches like miniature sky scrapers. He wraps them like a mother coddling her young and then places them safely in the refrigerator until the morning. This is a mindful exercise for him. He retreats for the night with a smile of anticipation for the feast that will nourish him the next day.

Practice

- » Build a sandwich with full awareness.
- » Use your senses of smell, touch, sight and sound.
- » Notice how your body reacts as you anticipate eating this sandwich.
- » Cut the sandwich in half to expose its layers.
- » Notice the colours and textures.
- » Take one bite.
- » Notice.
- » Eat slowly.

Pure happiness

It was a recommendation offered by a local, someone who knew the town and who would help us avoid the tourist traps and get a genuinely good meal. We arrived to the restaurant one half hour before the doors opened to assure getting a table. We lined up outside. At precisely 5 p.m. the door swung open, and the host welcomed us with a smile and a warm invitation to enter. The restaurant filled in minutes. A 1980's nostalgia soundtrack belted out songs by Bowie, Houston, Jackson, Wham and Madonna. Servers smiled, danced, and made helpful recommendations. The food was served, drinks were poured, and the room resonated pure happiness by both patrons and employees. Intention, attention, and attitude make for memorable experiences.

Practice

» Notice the difference when we or another truly give service with intention, attention and attitude.
» Service means "being with," recognizing all that each person brings, and the potential sacredness of the event.
» Notice the distinction.

A bad taste in my mouth

While on vacation, we sought out a well-deserved lunch. We wanted nutritious food, the kind with much texture, freshness, colour and good taste. We remembered having seen an advertisement about a restaurant with home-grown cuisine and unanimously agreed that this would be the place to eat. When we entered the premises, the owner verbally highlighted the day's features, but as she did this, she pulled each item wrapped in cellophane out of the freezer. This was not the freshness that we had anticipated. When we made a decision not to stay, she replied... "The fried food is down the street." She made a judgment, and as a prospective patron, it did not feel good. This left a bad taste in my mouth.

Practice

» Choose your words carefully today.
» If you're not sure what to say, stop, pause, listen, and then proceed.

The joy that licorice brings

Thich Nhat Hanh, author, poet and teacher, invites us to notice how quickly we react to anger. When we find ourselves becoming reactive and angry, he suggests that we:

1. Don't think
2. Don't act
3. Don't speak

I attempted to employ these mindfulness practices in my work setting, but was quickly pulled into workplace unhappiness. Our custodian, arrived to my office with a large container of red licorice. She thoughtfully shared it with all staff. In that moment, there were no malicious actions, no mention of office politics, and no unkind words. She provided opportunity for an impromptu sangha. We indulged in the experience, being with one another, eating red licorice.

Practice

» Can you create a safe space for a group to come together to share a treat?
» Does this provide an opportunity to build community?
» Notice what this invokes in you as the facilitator.
» Notice what this invokes in others.
» Notice what's changed, if anything (comradery, less tension, true presence).

Risotto comfort

When my Wise Wife and I are out of dinner options, we usually make up a risotto, a traditional Italian rice dish made from arborio rice. Hot stock or broth is slowly poured into the rice, a little at a time, allowing the liquid to be absorbed, resulting in a creamy, delicious comforting feast. Together, we made a sweet potato risotto. Previously, we made a mushroom Portobello concoction. Another time, it was a beet and blue cheese delight. After a grueling day at work, this dish offers warmth and comfort. It clings to your insides with its richness and texture. It invites you to bask in its comfort.

Practice

» Go to silence.
» Breathe.
» Check in with your thoughts, body sensations, and emotions.
» Ask yourself "What is called for now?"
» Find comfort.

The sweet, the savoury, and the tart

I dug out my mother's cookbook and flipped to the gum drop cake recipe that she used to make each Christmas. It is comprised of a light cinnamon flavoured batter filled with multi-coloured soft gummy candies that melt in your mouth. It calls for one cup of sugar, one cup of butter, and two cups of gum drops. In my wisdom, I thought I would modify it to make it seemingly healthier by today's standards. I replaced the butter with apple sauce. I cut the sugar in half and I was stingy with the gum drops. It turned out to be a huge disappointment – dry, crumbly, tasteless. Sometimes, in our zest to improve, we take it upon ourselves to redesign our lives. We want more peace. We want to get through discomfort and be more resilient in the end. We want to have less suffering. We want more materialism. But sometimes, we need to just be with life as it is. Altering it or forcing it to be a certain way might take away its richness and the important lessons to be learned. This includes the sweet, the savoury, and the tart aspects of it. The gum drop cake went into the garbage and I will try again another day.

Practice

- » Dig out an old family recipe.
- » Mindfully, place all ingredients out, taking your time to use all of your senses to notice.
- » Don't alter the recipe. Drop all expectations. Don't judge it as healthy or unhealthy.
- » Follow the recipe and trust that it will turn out as it has many times before.
- » Enjoy with full presence.

- 8 -

BEING MORE MINDFUL TO YOU

Taking time to meditate is not a waste of time. Meditating is essential to our wellbeing and one might argue that it is even life-giving. When we take time to touch inward, we are able to understand our compassionate self and this contributes to a sense of peace. In essence we become more comfortable in our own skin. We are able to embrace who we are and live in an authentic way. We develop a more intimate way of being with self and this resonates to those we are with.

Morning welcome

One calcium, one zinc, one vitamin C, one vitamin D, one cranberry tablet, and one probiotic capsule. Each night before bed, I carefully place this array of vitamins and supplements in a small glass container next to my coffee cup, the one with the bicycle on it, adjacent to the coffee maker. These multi-coloured pills have become my morning companions. I believe that they nurture my body and prevent physical breakdown. It is equally essential to nurture the mind. I set up my meditation cushion, my plaid wool blanket and my yoga mat for tomorrow morning's welcome. Now I can go to sleep, knowing that these gifts await and that I have done all that I could do for today.

Practice

- » Get ready for bed tonight with intention.
- » Set out your physical routine requirements.
- » Now the invitation is to plan how you will nurture your mind.
- » Set up what is required to do this.
- » When you shut off the light and go to bed, smile, breathe, and be thankful.

Authenticity

I finally did it. After twenty years, I purchased a new suit. My workplace attire is relatively casual. My work wardrobe consists of several crisply ironed cotton shirts with button down collars, comfortable leather oxfords, and a variety of khaki pants. I often reflect on having two shirts that I washed daily and ironed at the very beginning of my social work career, as money was tight and clothing was expensive back then. While working in healthcare, I have always gravitated to clothing that you could simply throw in the washer, hang to dry and wear, so the purchase of a new suit was something unusual for me.

As I walked into the men's fine clothing store with apprehension, I was greeted by a young man named Dillon. Within moments, he asked me to extend my arms as he measured me and handed me a suit jacket that fit like a glove. Within fifteen minutes, I was fitted and the suit was paid for. I dreaded what I had perceived would be a cumbersome task and was delighted with the ease of this entire process. Dillon is a master "suit smith." He is skilled and genuine, and it was because of this "authenticity" that the entire process went smoothly. It is important that we too are "authentic" if we want to provide the best service to those whom we serve. A large part of mindfulness is that its benefits are best discovered when we embody it whole-heartedly. It is easy to read much literature on the subject, conduct research, and hide behind knowledge and theory. This is all part of the doing rather than the being. Being fuels growth and awakens one's true nature.

Practice

- » Go to the cushion today.
- » No excuses.

Embracing all that we are

For the past five days, we have had an unexpected, but persistent visitor. From the crack of dawn until the sun sets, this black and indigo feathered starling has continually pecked away at our dining room window. We have attempted to frighten him by knocking on the window pane to no avail. We have pulled down blinds to diminish his reflection as we are convinced that he thinks that he has a friend or foe. And finally, we have welcomed him as another addition to our family. What does he see when he looks at his reflection? More importantly, what do we see when we look at our reflection in the mirror? Do we see layers of armour that we have clad in an attempt to carry on, or do we see complete openness exposing our true nature? We can hang on to safety or we can unmask our souls, discard our judgments and embrace the visitor within.

Practice

»   Take ten minutes of uninterrupted time to sit and look at yourself in the mirror.
»   Breathe.
»   What do you see? Notice without narration.
»   Breathe.

Break open the windows and let the fresh air in

The weather is a topic we often obsess about. We typically start our conversations by making reference to it either being too hot or too cold. No matter what the temperature, we often wish for it to be different. This past week has been marked by unseasonably warm temperatures. Brisk autumn days have been replaced with an influx of hazy, hot, and oppressive conditions. To deal with this intense heat, many have shut themselves in their homes and retreated to cool air-conditioned surroundings. Air conditioning initially feels good as it provides some relief and makes the heat tolerable. However, after a few days of breathing this artificial recirculated air, I long to break open the windows and let the fresh air in. The arrival of cooler temperatures allowed me to do this today. I noticed a difference to air quality. I could smell the freshness. I could hear the birds and crickets. It made me feel alive. Opening windows is a metaphor of how we come alive through the practice of mindfulness.

Practice

> » Breathe. Bring full awareness to the inbreath and the outbreath.
> » Notice with openness and spaciousness.
> » Open the window to what is happening internally and externally.
> » Notice.
> » Bask in this fresh way of being.

Silence

On a 7-day silent retreat, I gave up my mobile phone. No texting, no television, no reading, no music, and no internet. In the busyness of life, we are constantly multitasking and digitally connected. That makes an immersion into silence both daunting and exciting at the same time. An intentional opportunity for meditation and being with self.

Practice

> » Make a conscious choice to go to silence throughout your day.
> » Recognize that going to silence is one of the best gifts that you can give to yourself.

A purposeful pause

This past week I had the opportunity to participate in a silent mindfulness retreat. This immersion into silence challenged me to be with myself with no distraction. Sometimes, we need to remove ourselves to realize just how tired we are. We fall into autopilot and often fail to take the necessary time required to reflect on why we are doing what we are doing. Are our activities still fueling our passion? Are we still finding joy and satisfaction? Are we contributing to a better society?

Practice

> » Pause.
> » Breathe.
> » Touch inward.
> » Be honest with self.
> » Use your wisdom to move forward in a gentle way.

The gift bag

Every Christmas, my Wise Wife digs out her favourite gift bag that our youngest daughter, Brown Eyes, made for her at the age of five. Brown Eyes had a teacher who helped her transform an ordinary paper shopping bag into a Christmas gift bag. The bag is painted and adorned with a red paper cut-out cardinal and glued-on sunflower seeds. It has become a coveted yearly treasure. Time has lapsed, seeds have fallen off, Brown Eyes is now a teacher herself, and it continues to be special. When we take time to meditate, we discover unexpected treasures. Discovery of these precious gifts offers us stability and assurance.

Practice

» Take a few moments today to go to contemplation and stillness.
» Treasure all that is there.

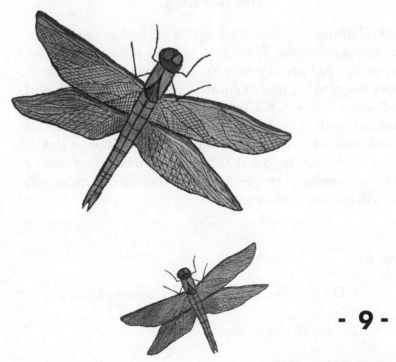

- 9 -

THIS MOMENT

We often miss much of our life as we are absorbed with thinking about the past or worrying about the future. Our default mode is one of constant rumination. Our mind is filled with much chatter, even when we try to go to stillness. It is a monkey mind, constantly jumping from one thought to the next, like monkeys swing from tree to tree. We find it difficult to be satisfied with where we are when we are here. We want for bigger, better, richer and so on, and we miss out on this moment. Life does not have to be filled with novelty. We can be content in everyday existence. Mindfulness encourages us to be open to all of life's offerings.

This makes me happy

"Do you think we could meditate today?" The words were sincere and poignant. They struck a chord in my heart. They oozed out of a patient during an interview at the end of a day, at the end of a work week. This patient has had longstanding depression and was introduced to the practice of mindfulness two years ago. There is less regret for past events and less apprehension about tomorrow. There is more self-compassion. The patient shares that the past three years have been the happiest that they remember. This makes me happy. My response is "Of course, I always have time to meditate." As I sit with my hands on my thighs in stillness and the patient and I both arrive to the breath, I am grateful for this opportunity.

Practice

> »   Extend this same invitation to yourself.
> »   "Do you think we could meditate today?"
> »   Find a quiet space and sit mindfully, with gratitude.

Homeostasis

Lights out. Last good nights exchanged. The house is calm. The moon is full. For the moment, I will savour this peacefulness. It is not permanent and life circumstances can change at any time. The old rituals. The daily grind. Homeostasis. Enjoy.

Practice

» When you turn off the last light tonight, on your way to
bed, stop and pause.
» Breathe.
» Bring your full awareness to this moment.
» Notice what is happening internally and externally.
» Allow the breath to ground you.
» Proceed.

Mindfulness is like the sunshine

After the cold of winter, sunshine becomes a welcomed ally in the
spring. Allow yourself to soak it in. Allow it to pour into every
nook and cranny of your mind and body, making you feel alive and
waking you up from the lethargies of your existence. Allow for it
to illuminate your pathway and give you a new lens from which
to see the world around you, a world with more clarity, hope, and
compassion. Let it settle in your consciousness, comfort you, and
give you all of its nourishment to sustain you when the storm
clouds roll in. Mindfulness is like the sun. Drink it. Allow it to
warm your bones.

Practice

» Find a comfortable seat in the sun.
» In stillness, allow the sun to warm you.
» Just be.

Today, I will choose to be gentle with myself

The alarm sounds and I lay motionless in bed. Could it really be time to get up to go to work? Where did the night with its starry skies and dreams of flying and gastronomical delights go? Mindfulness suggests that we seize the moment. For this moment is all that we have. Right now, I would like to seize many moments and go back to sleep! The time change has played havoc with my circadian rhythms which are governed by my body's biological clock. Today, I will choose to be gentle with myself until my body catches up to the rest of the world.

Practice

» Today's invitation is to be gentle with yourself.

Unravelling

A long day, multiple commitments, many clients with complex needs. I just wanted to get home, put my feet up and relax. Then arrived a text from my daughter, Blue Eyes. She advised that her plan for the evening entailed baking chocolate chip cookies and she wanted to know if I would like to visit, have a cup of tea, and get caught up on news. It would have been so easy to decline her invitation, but I knew that spending time with her would be wonderful, no matter what we did. Truth be told, I miss this time and treasure every opportunity that I get to be with my children. Sometimes, we need to stretch ourselves. It is easy to get caught up in the everyday tasks, but it is so life giving to take advantage of precious opportunities when they knock at our door.

Practice

» As your day unfolds, be open to the unravelling and precious opportunities.

Seize the day

I was awakened to the sound of robins chirping. One particular robin taps on our living room window every morning. I could not figure out why he would do this for hours on end, but today, it struck me. The bird's tapping nudges me to wake up, be thankful, and seize the day.

This week I unexpectedly met three of my previous patients. We struck up conversations and it felt wonderful to see them again. I couldn't help but notice how much they had changed. The young person who came to my office years ago with a spark in their eyes was now quite compromised. The young teen that was rebellious and attractive was now older and indifferent. The person who used to run up the stairwell and pick wild blueberries was now frail and struggling. Seize the moment my friends. The robin is telling us something.

Practice

» Be open to subtle invitations to seize this moment.

Just a regular day

You never know how your day is going to unfold. When I woke up yesterday morning, I had my coffee, packed my running gear and walked to work, fully anticipating just a regular day. At about 10:00 a.m. my Wise Wife called to advise that her elderly father was on his way to the hospital. This is the second time in one week. I cleared my work schedule, rushed home to pack, and we hopped in the car for the six hour drive to be with him. After driving for about an hour, we received a call that he was fine, was stabilized, and being sent home. He would be cared for and not alone. We were advised to turn around and return home. It was a roller coaster of emotions and events. I can appreciate how quickly life can change. Mindfulness can help us to navigate through life.

Practice

- » Breathe.
- » Notice its ever-changing nature.
- » Notice that like each moment, each breath has its unique qualities.
- » No one breath is better than another.
- » We just breathe.
- » Similarly, no one moment is better than the other.
- » We live, being in this moment...and this moment...and this moment.

Choice

The alarm goes off. I lay there for a moment listening to the silence, the gentle sound of the rain, birds chirping. I catch a whiff of the fresh coffee grounds sitting in the filter inviting my arrival. I could let my monkey mind go to the lists of things to be done, the unsavoury nature of the cold, darkness and rain, the grass in the backyard that needs to be cut, and the fact I need to get to work. But in this moment, I choose to savour life and whatever unfolds on this day with the realization that I have choice.

Practice

> » When you wake up in the morning, simply arrive and check in.
> » Breathe.
> » Notice how easy it is for the mind to spiral and get caught up in negativity.
> » Realize you have choice.

Anticipation

There's excitement in the air each morning as the light peaks in through the cracks of the blinds gently nudging me to wake up. It arrives as a warm invitation to enjoy each moment with presence and curiosity. It calls me to be grateful and to not get swept into the tides of sadness. It reminds me to be appreciative for all that I have. Indigenous author/playwright/poet, Tomson Highway suggests that when we wake up each morning, that we give thanks for a heart that beats, eyes that see, legs that walk. Like a child on Christmas morning, I delight in making my way to the gifts that lay before me, soon to be revealed.

Practice

- » Breathe.
- » Be thankful for this body as it is in this moment.
- » Begin with walking meditation. *
- » Place one foot in front of the next.
- » Notice the sensation of the foot rising and falling with each step.
- » Take time to stop, to curiously notice one object.
- » Notice what draws you to this object.
- » Anticipate, just being fully with it, using all of your senses.
- » Notice how this feels.
- » Linger. Explore that object with openness and pay attention to what unfolds, if anything.
- » After some time, move on to another object that invites your attention.
- » Continue this practice.
- » Take time to reflect on how it felt to look at the world this way.

*If it is not possible for you to physically walk, you can do this practice in a sitting posture.

He finally popped the question!

As we were preparing dinner, and while Brown Eyes had left the kitchen, he said "I would like to ask you a question...Do you think it would be alright if I were to marry your daughter?" Completely taken off guard, we stopped what we were doing and hugged him with delight. He then signaled us to quickly take cover in a nearby closet. As we were huddled in the closet, he reached his long lean arm upwards in a contorted fashion and grabbed the hidden diamond engagement ring and proudly showed us. He is an honest, hardworking, loveable young man, and most importantly, he loves our Brown Eyes. Mindfulness is about gentle inquiry. Stopping and taking a moment to ask yourself the question "How do I choose to live my life in this moment?" Lean in with open heart and eyes.

Practice

» Find yourself comfortably seated, hands resting on thighs, back erect and dignified, jaw relaxed pointing slightly downward, feet firmly planted, gaze softened or eyes closed.

» Notice both inbreath and outbreath.

» Notice the pressure points of your body...feet touching ground...hands touching thighs...buttocks touching chair...etc.

» Notice the sensation of clothes touching body, skin touching air.

» Notice the weather of the mind...settled or stormy?

» If your mind wanders, gently bring it back to body and breath. Note that this is okay.

» Now pop the question?

» Do I want to live in this moment with full awareness?

» Go forward with full luminosity.

Today's Island

It is easy to conceptualize the notion of living in the moment mindfully, but sometimes, this is difficult to do. We needlessly gravitate to the past with memories, regrets, and scrutiny. We frequently worry about tomorrow with dreams, hopes, and aspirations. Living on each end of this spectrum, past and future, prevents us from being here right now. While on a mindfulness retreat, our teacher suggested that, upon awakening each morning, we visualize being in a boat that has just landed on an island. The island is symbolic of a single day. It is open for curious exploration, and yet, it has boundaries that prevent us from navigating beyond. When our minds begin to race to the future, we simply need to remind ourselves that we are on today's island, and tomorrow, we will have sufficient time to "be with" tomorrow's island. Today's island is a precious gift, just waiting to be explored.

Practice

- » Treat each day as an island.
- » Yesterday's island is long behind, no longer accessible by boat.
- » Tomorrow's island is distant and not yet visible to the eye.
- » Be here, right now, on this island.
- » If your mind wanders, allow for the breath to anchor you to this moment.

Let go

As I walked in the park last week, I witnessed a little boy who spouted off "look at me, daddy, I'm a big boy." As he sat on the swing and his father pushed him, he opened his arms outward, let go of the swing, and rocketed thought the air, landing safely on his two feet. In this moment, he displayed complete trust, full awareness, and genuine delight. I hope that you can do the same today.

Practice

» Find yourself standing with eyes closed.
» Drop into the body and the breath with full awareness.
» Notice all of its parts working in unison to keep you upright.
» Be attuned to how you are feeling.
» Next, open your arms, extending them outwards and upwards, honouring your body with kindness and non-judgment.
» Allow for your body to move very gently, swaying instinctually.
» No need to steer it a certain way.
» Just be with it now.
» Let go.

I will jump in those sprinklers

A heat wave has settled over most of Ontario and parts of the northern USA. The sun is scorching. You could proverbially fry an egg on the sidewalk. People are fatigued from the heat and lack of sleep, and tempers are reactive. Lawns have transitioned from lush green to straw yellow, and sprinklers and watering hoses are attempting to quench the parched earth's thirst. People on the elevators are complaining of the unforgiving heat. Ironically, these are the same people that complained this past winter about the cold weather, anxious for summer to arrive. When can we simply enjoy the moment as it is with all of its scars and blemishes? Tomorrow, I will get up early so I can get out for a morning run, to beat the heat of sunrise. I will jump in those sprinklers and bask in the cool relief that they offer. I will let the water quench my dry skin. I will whistle, hum to music, and playfully raise my arms in a sun salutation when I stretch and reach for the sky.

Practice

- » Go outside.
- » Allow yourself to be fully present with your surroundings.
- » Snow...wind...sun...rain...breeze.
- » Embrace it in a playful way, with new eyes.
- » Notice.

Seeing clearly

The sky turned black as the thunderstorm moved in. We dashed for the car and drove to find the girls on their paper route with much trepidation anticipating the worst. Our two daughters, Brown Eyes and Blue Eyes, were delivering papers and we were worried about their safety as the storm intensified. Upon turning the corner, we spotted them through a thick curtain of rain. Blue Eyes was pulling Brown Eyes sitting in the red wagon, propped on a stack of newspapers, holding a ladybug umbrella. They were no worse for wear. So indicative of how our minds catastrophize. The left side of our brain creates complicated storylines that are not always accurate, and this causes us much stress and reactivity.

Practice

» Take a few moments to give yourself a well-deserved purposeful pause today.
» See beyond the blankets of rain.

Hidden passage

Each morning, I cut through a pathway in a park. A fence encircles the park boundary, but if you look closely, through a clump of overgrown lilac bushes, you can see a part of the fence with a couple of boards missing and has become a makeshift passageway. I often marvel at what lies on the other side of that fence. My imagination contemplates the wonderland beyond. For me, this resonates how we often live our lives. We experience daily events looking for that escape, that distraction, that passageway to perceived solace. In doing so, we miss the majesty of the moment, right here, right now.

Practice

» Take a moment in your busy day to explore how your desires to be elsewhere preclude you from enjoying this present moment.
» Notice, without judgement, how often your mind takes you off down an alternate pathway.

» When this happens, look for an object nearby to touch. It could be a leaf, flower, desk, doorway, etc.
» Let this touch help you to come back to now.

Monotony

Morning alarm...coffee...walk...work...home...dinner...bed. Seems so gloomy and repetitive. Greyness has emerged, and the blues and greens of the summer palate have departed for autumn. The mornings and evenings are less inviting. Turning the furnace up one degree at a time to ward off the chill, we just can't get warm enough. Without the light, we struggle to stay awake past 9 p.m., only to start all over again tomorrow. Such monotony as winter begins to knock at our door. The ebbs and flows of life, from one season to the next, from hot to cold. Embrace it all.

Practice

» The next time you feel bored, stay with it.
» Explore its duration, frequency, triggers, and intensity.
» Notice the tendency to distract or avoid.
» Understand that boredom is a part of being human.
» Being with boredom, as being with excitement, cultivates equanimity.

Splendour of the moment

I had the privilege of being in the Colorado mountains attending a week-long silent retreat. It was magical. Snow created a winter wonderland. Each morning, I would leave the comfort of our room, go outside to another building to bring back two cups of coffee. Each morning, I watched the sun rise against the backdrop of the Rocky Mountains. The people were inspiring and memorable, and the entire experience was life-changing. A year later, I found myself reminiscing about the retreat and feeling this year seemed less exciting. My youngest daughter, Brown Eyes, has left the nest empty. My Wise Wife has just left her work to pursue new pathways. My body is one year older and aches in places that I didn't even know existed. But in an instant, my melancholy was altered with the surprise news that our eldest daughter, Blue Eyes, was engaged. So, just when I thought it couldn't get better, life turned around to remind me that it could.

Practice

>> Look for splendour in the moment in all that you say and do.
>> In times of upheaval and in times of peace, embrace it all.

Blessed

We were up at 3 a.m., into a taxi at 4:30 a.m., and on the plane at 6 a.m. We were to connect in Toronto...then in Denver...then to have reached our destination of Anchorage, Alaska by sundown. However, we were only on the first leg of the trip, arriving in Toronto, and it all went amuck. We became trapped in line at customs with hundreds of other travelers, many desperately trying to make their flight connections. The staff in yellow jackets were incredibly detached and they corralled us as we individually pleaded for them to call our destination and move us to the front of the line. Passengers were huffing and rolling their eyes in frustration. Minute by minute, time lapsed and we came to realize we were not going to make our flight.

In the midst of this chaos we connected in another way, a human way. The lady ahead of us busted out her iPad and began to show us her photos of the music class she taught. The guy in front of her, with the Bostonian accent, offered us unconditional hope. The couple with the four children smiled as the children entertained us. Eventually, we came to a yellow coated staff who spoke to us about the theme of gratitude. She helped us to realize that such trivial airport nonsense should not be allowed to spoil our day. She spoke of being blessed even as passengers scoffed at her in line. She spoke of knowing that people in line were sending loving kindness to strangers even if they did not realize it.

This was a mindfulness lesson at its finest. All we could do was surrender to the moment, drop the judgment, the "should haves" and "could haves," and to simply just be. Mindfulness means accepting the whole that life throws your way.

Practice

> » The next time you are travelling, take a few moments to notice what is happening around you.
> » Public transportation venues (train stations, bus terminals, subway lines) are wonderful places to be mindful.
> » Explore faces.
> » Listen to the sounds...people talking, engines running,

agents assisting patrons.
» Observe the people who work there.
» Pay attention to the interactions.
» Notice scents, sounds, temperatures.
» Notice what's happening in your body as you do this.
» Breathe.

The last breath

Sitting in the ICU unit with my mother hooked up to life support gives a whole new meaning to living in the moment. The sounds... mechanical alarms against the backdrop of the rhythmical ventilator; the busyness of health care professionals skirmishing around the unit; and the utterances of the patient across the hall trying to free himself from his bed, pulling off his oxygen mask and cursing vulgarities. I was aware of the multitude of injections for pain, infection, blood pressure regulation. The arrival and departure of the final breath.

Practice

» Take a few moments to honour the gift of the breath if you are feeling overwhelmed today.
» The gift of the breath is more significant than we will ever fully know.

- 10 -

ESSENCE OF CHANGE

I have purposefully sequenced these stories and insights according to season, to subtly illustrate change. Recently, a participant in a mindfulness program shared with me their realization that change will always be. The participant elaborated that change is often abrupt, unforgiving, and in many ways, necessary. She further elaborated that mindfulness has been a tool for her to cope with change and to feel more resilient in situations that feel uncomfortable or out of control. Living in the north helps us to be fully aware of change as we experience the four seasons, and develop an unwavering resilience to these transitions as solid as our rocky landscape. Change will happen. Mindfulness helps us to be with it in curiosity and know that we have the inner resources required to weather it.

New beginnings

The full moon that lit up our dark nights and gave sparkle to the snow has now moved on. A new white snowfall has brightened up our surroundings and the brilliant sunshine has erased the grey that has hovered over us the past two months. This year's Christmas tree is discarded outside and all the decorations that adorned it are now tucked away for next year. My eldest daughter's suitcase is packed and sits near the garage door. That suitcase will depart with her on Friday as she embarks on the continuation of her out-of-town post graduate studies. The new Dalai Lama tear-off calendar with inspiring quotes for the upcoming New Year sits next to the fresh ground coffee and mugs that will greet me tomorrow morning as I prepare to return to work. We are fortunate to have so many new beginnings. They help us to move from the past and to awaken to the present moment.

Practice

> » Today, be aware of new beginnings.

Still

The clocks have gone ahead one hour and many people are still floundering, trying to adapt to a new normal. I hear them talk about being exhausted. Some can't get to sleep, claiming it is just too early. Others want to hang on to the past few weeks when the sunlight graced the mornings, not fond of the return to dark. The darkness and light in our lives are constantly changing.

Both are gentle reminders of impermanence. When we go to stillness, through the practice of mindfulness, we can be with it all. This is equanimity.

Practice

» Go to stillness.
» Be in this moment.
» Embrace impermanence.

An illusion of safety

While running on a sidewalk adjacent to a busy roadway, I realized that the only thing that separates me from that roadway is the six-foot snowbank. This snowbank stands tall, giving the illusion of safety. We frequently go through much of our life confident in our own false fortresses of security. As I put one step in front of the other, I came to the realization that life can change at any moment. Nothing is permanent. The wall that stands to protect us, whether self-created, or built by society, is only an illusion of safety. Are you brave enough to take down that wall and expose your vulnerability? Are you brave enough to understand that there is no me or them? Mindfulness helps us to understand that walls are illusions. There is only a we.

Practice

» Take a moment to breathe.
» Reflect. Are there barriers that you have created to be

safe? To protect you?
» Breathe.
» Now let go.

Just as it should be

Brown Eyes is chatting with her boyfriend, both immersed in helping each other through college assignments. Blue Eyes is chatting with university friends thousands of kilometers to the west. Belly laughter emerges from her room. My Wise Wife is tucked under the covers, hopefully having sweet dreams. I am enjoying the moment and trusting that everything is in place just as it should be. Sometimes, we just have to trust and let things be. This is a hard task for many of us who like to be in control. Mindfulness helps us surrender to change. This assists with accepting things just as they are.

Practice

» Allow for things to be just as they are.
» Notice.
» Trust.

Tango of nature

Have you ever paid attention to the patterns of emergence and retreat? I have witnessed this phenomenon as the snow retreats only to return again in a rhythmical manner until its eventual exodus. It is a tango of nature, with a lead and a follower, partners in dance. We see this pattern in the trajectory of life – an emergence of stability followed by an abrupt change marked with unpredictability and turmoil. Water flows into shore and retreats eroding all that is in its path. The in-breath emerges and the out-breath retreats. This pattern is natural to our existence.

Practice

» Take some time to notice the ebbs and flows in your life.

Safe passages

My youngest daughter, Brown Eyes, is contemplating leaving home. She is a fine young woman who is striving for her independence as part of the natural cycle in life, having just completed her undergraduate degree. At twenty-one years of age, she can make these decisions, but interestingly, the other night, she asked my Wise Wife and me to sit down to "have a conversation." She prefaced the discussion by telling us how much she loved us and how happy she has been at home. She spoke of her intentions which were responsible and admirable. This was followed by her stating that she would like our approval as it was important for her to have this support. It dawned on me the importance of being heard, understood, and supported. Many come to us seeking our approval. They want to be accepted for who they are. They want to be acknowledged as being unique with their own hopes and fears. Perhaps the best gift that we can give them is to offer them impartiality, compassion, and the opportunity to make safe passage.

Practice

» Take a moment to reflect on a person or persons who are struggling with a decision.
» Pay attention to your own thoughts and biases.
» Notice how they influence your perception of the situation.
» Talk less and listen more.
» Be an impartial witness.
» Be kind.

Transitions

My youngest daughter, Brown Eyes, graduates from university this week. This is a peak moment. The day will be ceremonial and full of much emotion as she embarks on another life transition. It will be a celebration of much love and pride as we stand on the sidelines cheering her on. Change is non-linear. Each change requires adjustment and acceptance. Mindfulness makes these transitions easier to navigate. Mindfulness is that companion that supports you from the sidelines.

Practice

» Peak moments occur when we are fully immersed in events unfolding in front of us.

» Peak moments invite us to be completely present, using all of our senses.
» Bring to mind a peak moment in your life.
» Embrace it with full lumiosity.

Cheers Brown Eyes!

My youngest, Brown Eyes, has just been hired to teach twenty-two seven-year old children at the other end of the country. She is a natural in the classroom, and sure to inspire and cultivate self-worth and wisdom, two important qualities that are often missing in adults that I see in my daily practice. I know this new job is an opportunity for her growth, and in my heart of hearts, I know she is doing the right thing by accepting this position. I can feel this in my body. My pulse is not elevated. My chest is not tight. My breathing does not feel constricted. There is no yukky feeling in my belly. I believe this feeling of inner peace will help all of us to adjust over the next few months, during this exciting but heartfelt transition. Being comfortable with our decisions, no matter how difficult or turbulent they may be, helps us to move forward. As long as we are settled in ourselves, we are able to bring out our best. Going to the cushion to meditate allows for us to stop, pay attention, and then to proceed with confidence and wisdom.

Practice

» We often rely on books and the internet to direct us.
» If you are faced with a difficult decision put those resources away.
» Go to the breath.
» Pay attention to what is happening in your body and be

open to its wisdom.

» Trust in your intuition to make the right decision.
» Don't look to the past or get preoccupied with the future.
» Pay attention to what is called for now.

Stable, solid and grounding

While visiting my office today, a patient commented about my rock collection sitting on the far left corner of my desk. We shared our fascination with rocks and spoke of how we both acquired them from places travelled. A gifted rock from a previous patient. A smooth round rock painted like a ladybug from my youngest daughter Brown Eyes. A flat rock with a painted campfire scene. My home is also adorned with these familiar companions from Australia to the Bay of Fundy. They offer me comfort. Time passes and no matter what changes in my life, they remain stable, solid, and grounding.

Practice

» Find a small rock.
» Notice what has drawn you to it.
» Place it in your pocket and carry it with you.
» When you feel overwhelmed by emotions or events, place your hand in your pocket and touch it. This is a simple mindfulness practice that you can do anywhere, anytime.
» Let it anchor you to the present moment.

Imagine freedom

The morning glory budded its first sapphire blue blossom yesterday. My running paths are laced with white textured Queen Anne's Lace. The pop-up greenhouse at our neighbourhood grocery store parking lot has been constructed and taken down. There is change in the air. I feel it. It's not the kind of change that gnaws at your stomach or causes trepidation. It is a more curious happening, a revealing. Imagine if we could simply let things be. Then we could observe with curiosity rather than angst. Imagine the freedom.

Practice

> » Stop, breathe and observe.
> » Is there change in the air?
> » Can you be open and curious to it?

Where did our summer go?

The mountain ash berries are slowly evolving to crimson. The first morning glory trumpet shaped blossom arrived. The mornings are already cooler and patio solar lanterns are still aglow as I make the coffee and glance out the kitchen window. My Wise Wife utters "Where did our summer go?" with bewilderment. Nothing stays the same. The universe around us is in constant flux. Rather than trying to make sense of it, see if you can simply just allow it to be.

Practice

> » We frequently complain about change.

» Weather and seasons changing often take a lot of negative space.
» This change in weather happens annually. It is what it is.
» The next time you feel inclined to speak negatively about these changes, catch yourself.
» Don't over analyze.
» Don't hang on to what was.
» Don't wish it to be different.
» Smile.
» Let it be.

Left behind

We experienced a family death. This was abrupt, unexpected, and final. We went through traditional visitation ritual and funeral service. Emotions were raw. It is an unintended send off. The priest took the podium. He did not know the deceased. He spoke of pain for those left behind, how this was not a goodbye but simply a transition to a new existence. I found his words to be comforting. He did not embellish this with talk of angels and a better place. He simply spoke of a new way of being. There are times in our life when we too might feel left behind. We don't need to fix this or make it different. We simply need to be in touch with how it resonates within us and let it be.

Practice

» Take a mindful moment to reflect on a time when you felt left behind.
» What were the challenges you faced?
» How did it resonate in your body, thoughts, and

emotions?
- » What was it you wanted in this situation?
- » What did you actually get?
- » What did you learn from this experience?
- » Does the practice of mindfulness have a role to play in future situations when you might feel left behind?

Do you have an emotional attachment to this tooth?

A tooth ache following an unsuccessful filling brought me to my dentist. My dentist usually asks me "Do you have an emotional attachment to this tooth?" which is often indicative that things do not look good. I always answer "YES!" But attachment is viewed as the root of all suffering. How paradoxical when you consider this. I am attached to my tooth, even though it pains me presently. So often we attach ourselves to our storyline. We attach ourselves to who we believe we are and what we do. So, are we prepared for the moment when we become detached? If the tooth is removed, will my suffering cease? It is important that we stay open minded and not become rigid in our thinking. Nothing is clearly right or clearly wrong and we must cast aside all conclusions. I still have my tooth and I am not about to give up on it quite yet.

Practice

- » Complete this sentence... "I have an emotional attachment to..."
- » This inquiry can be applied to many aspects of our life.
- » Notice with awareness.

» Does this attachment contribute to suffering?
» Be open to exploring change.

The move

During the weekend, we moved our daughter, Blue Eyes, and her future husband into a lovely new home. It was a coming together of two families and dear friends, determined to make the transition as smooth as possible for this young couple. An act of love that involved scrubbing floors, moving furniture, unpacking boxes, and assembling beds. We gave unselfishly, completely. That evening, we gathered around the table for great food, much laughter, tears, and wine. It was a memorable celebration, a milestone.

Practice

» Consider a time in your life when you transitioned. It may have been a home, a job, a community, etc.
» Consider current transitions, day to day, task to task, moment to moment.
» Acknowledge the skill, strength, and awareness that is required to withstand change.
» Celebrate change.

Maneuverability

"Mom, do I cook the pasta first and then add it to the cheese ingredients or do I cook it all together?" uttered Brown Eyes by telephone from afar. "Do I use bread crumbs on top or not?" "Do I cook it in the same pot and then just put it in the oven?"

The recipe for macaroni and cheese is pretty precise, but when I make it, I often improvise, throwing in spinach or broccoli and whatever else I can find in the fridge to make it healthier. I believe that recipes are meant to be guides. They usually have some degree of maneuverability. They are not set in stone. We must keep this in mind with life expectations. The ingredients of our life may fluctuate and be altered. When we allow for flexibility, we learn to improvise through life's challenges. This provides a recipe for better living.

Practice

> » Many of us like to be in control and have precision about the direction of our life.
> » Do you craft out strategic recipes, to assure things turning out a certain way?
> » How do you cope when an ingredient changes or is not available?
> » What patterns of behaviour emerge as part of your default mode of operating?
> » Is there rigidity or flexibility?
> » How does this impact your reaction?
> » Breathe.
> » Notice.

Do I keep going?

Every summer, we rent a cottage. I map out my run which usually entails a jaunt down an old abandoned railway track filled with views of pines, white granite mountains, and deep blue lakes. At kilometer three, I come face to face with an abandoned railway bridge with wooden trestles. Beneath is a turbulent river and waterfall. Do I keep going and cross those open wooden planks or do I turn around and go back?

We often face troubling times when we would like to turn around and go back to safety, but are unable. Times when you know that orchestrating change might necessitate opening old wounds. It would be so safe and easy to turn back to a place of predictability, but you persevere. Rather than exploring we can easily be swept away by distraction, only skimming the surface. The practice of mindfulness helps you to be with self with enhanced presence, clarity, and kindness. This is vital to getting safely to the other side of change.

Practice

- » Pause.
- » Don't turn back.
- » Holding on creates suffering.
- » Keep going with clarity, wisdom, and kindness.

Transitional times

The evenings are darker and quieter. The lull of children playing and dogs barking has been replaced with the rattling of leaves and an anticipation of autumn. A thick dew covers the grass each morning. The snooze bar on my iPhone gets a dusting off each morning with increased usage. The leaves are beginning to change colour and fall. Change is inevitable. We cannot control it. When we attempt to grasp or cling to the past, we suffer. These are transitional times. This is the way it is meant to be.

Practice

- » When you awaken each morning take a moment to pay attention to your body, thoughts, and emotions.
- » Notice these as they are now.
- » Look out of the window.
- » Notice. Look for obvious and subtle changes.
- » Accept that change is inevitable.
- » Do it all over again the next day.

Permanent markers

In the third class of the Mindfulness-Based Stress Reduction program, we post a large plasticized diagram of a human body on the wall. We then engage class participants in a discussion about recent pleasant and unpleasant events. Their comments and insights about thoughts, body sensations, and emotions are written down – posted for all to see. The diagram is a nice visual on this topic of stress reactivity.

Immediately following this class, I proceeded to erase the written comments on this diagram, realizing I had accidently used permanent markers instead of dry erase. One of the key themes of this class is impermanence. Suffering is intensified when we resist change. I quietly chuckle at the irony of this mishap – permanent markers to illustrate the theme of impermanence.

Practice

- » Pause. Breathe. Arrive in this moment.

» Draw an outline of a human body.
» Reflect on a recent pleasant or unpleasant event.
» Write down on the diagram, your thoughts, feelings, and body sensations.
» Breathe.
» Realize the impermanent nature of it all.

Smooth white pencil lines among your deep blue sky

Have you ever taken the time to look up to see a jet gliding through the sky? The lingering "jet trail" usually appears as a distinct white line, as if someone had taken a large white pencil and marked up the blue background. Onlookers often marvel at this image while wondering where the jet has come from and where it is heading. The next time that you embark on a new journey know that you too can leave the past behind and proceed with a clean slate. Smooth white pencil lines are among your deep blue sky. It is an opportunity for a new beginning.

Practice

» The next time a jet goes by, stop, look up, and notice.
» Pay attention to the white exhaust line that follows.
» Notice its initial intensity, and how it fades and becomes more diffused with time.
» Notice how it eventually completely disappears.
» Realize that things may come and things may go, and that you can still be here through all of this change.
» Embrace an opportunity to move forward with a clean slate.

OBSTACLES IN YOUR

MEDITATION PRACTICE

When participants initially sign up for mindfulness training, they frequently arrive with an illusion that mindfulness awareness will be easy to attain. Once in the program, however, they come to realize that this is difficult work that requires a great deal of patience and commitment.

Some participants may drop out of the program as they struggle with making time to practice as well as encountering other obstacles that get in the way of meditating. Whether participating in a mindfulness program or learning the practice of mindfulness independently, we may face many of the same obstacles. Common obstacles in meditation may include falling asleep, boredom, agitation, or the challenges of the wandering mind. Some expect that mindfulness practice will rid them of unpleasantness or ruminating thoughts. Some judge and are hard on themselves in the process. Obstacles are completely normal. It is important to exercise flexibility with practice as well as to be kind and gentle to self. Mindfulness is not about passing or failing. It is about just being.

"But I have no time to meditate"

I am always amazed to hear people say "I don't have time to meditate." Many of us want to feel better, have more control over our life, and respond with emotional intelligence. We want to live life to the fullest, in the present moment, yet we react with hesitation when asked to set aside fifteen minutes of our day to nurture our mind. While visiting a pharmacy recently, I was amazed to count eighteen shelves of "fix me ups," "maintenance kits," and "make over cosmetics", reinforcing our obsession with body. Mindfulness practice plays a huge role in nurturing our mind. It does this by re-structuring the grey matter of the brain through a process referred to as neuroplasticity. It strengthens neuron pathways. The mind deserves the same amount of attention that the body seems to get. Making time to meditate is essential for our wellbeing.

Practice

>> Schedule 15 minutes a day to engage in formal mindfulness practice (body scan, sitting meditation, walking meditation, eating mindfully, gentle yoga, etc.).
>> Build this into a time of day that will be most conducive to you achieving this goal. This might be first thing in the morning upon waking, upon initial arrival to work, at lunch hour or possibly immediately following dinner.
>> Mindfulness is about wakefulness, so make sure that you avoid times of the day when you are more tired, and likely to fall asleep.
>> Prioritize this as being important.
>> Ask your family and friends for their support.
>> Be realistic and don't over strive. Start slow with genuine intention and commitment.

Sit with it

There's nowhere to put it. The snow has continued to bury us. Shoveling the driveway now requires throwing the snow as high as possible over a seven-foot snow bank. Sidewalks have become swamp-like with each and every step being laborious. There is pleasantness in the snow's beauty and unpleasantness in its amount and its unforgiving persistence. At times in our life, we feel completely saturated. We wonder just how much more we can take? There's simply no more room in our already burdened lives. Nowhere to put more pain and anguish. The piles are high enough. So, there becomes no other alternative but to simply sit with it.

Practice

» Are chores, responsibilities, self-expectations, and expectations of others overwhelming?

» How does this resonate with you physically, emotionally and in your thought processes?

» When you attempt to meditate does it feel like your mind is full and jumping from worry to worry.

» Can you accept that minds think? This is normal.

» Bring your awareness back to the breath, when your mind slips into this default mode of wandering.

» Know that this is just part of the practice.

» Understand that the wandering mind is an unhappy mind.

Wetland of worry

While snowshoeing, my future son-in-law went through the ice. He sunk in frozen marsh to the point that his leg was trapped four feet under and his head poked up above two feet of snow on the surface. He was trapped. With persistent maneuvering, he was able to free his foot from his snowshoe and, with the help of a rope and snowmobile, he was able to be rescued. When we made an inquiry the next day, we were told that he should not have been snowshoeing on the marsh because these grassy wetlands never freeze. There is always something stirring below the surface, just like our thoughts, an unsettledness. The practice of mindfulness keeps us from sinking in this endless wetland of worry.

Practice

» The mind is always thinking.
» Notice.
» Gently and firmly bring your awareness back to the breath.
» The mind is always thinking.
» Notice.
» Gently and firmly bring your awareness back to the breath.
» The mind is always thinking.
» Notice.
» Gently and firmly bring your awareness back to the breath.

Time out

If you drive up Regent Street, in my home community, and look up at the hospital sign perched on thirty feet of granite cliffs, you may notice my silhouette sitting on the cement foundation in a meditation lotus posture. I usually make my way to this location at noon hour each day. There is really nowhere else to escape for me during my workday to sit in stillness. It provides me with background noise to explore with curiosity, fresh air to breathe, and sunshine to warm up. It has become a special place that I can go to for time out and stillness.

Practice

> » Find a special place that will help you to maintain your daily meditation practice.
> » It does not have to be perfect. It just needs to be comfortable and inviting.
> » Make it your own.

Full potential

The pop-up greenhouse has found its way back to our local grocery store parking lot and is overflowing with garden greenery. It invites us to seize the moment, select our bedding plants, and transform our yard into a sanctuary. We will work intensely from sunrise to the dinner hour. We will remove debris, map out a landscaping plan, mix soil, spread peat moss, and dig. We will put our hands into soil, rotating it to make way for new delights. In the end, we will stand back and marvel at what we have accomplished. Our bodies will be sore and tired, but content. Now the difficult part.

We will sit back and allow plants to grow, without rushing them, trusting in their ability to reach full potential with water, sunshine, and gentleness. We can adapt these same principles in cultivating our mindfulness.

Practice

- » Plant the seeds for your meditation practice.
- » Provide the necessities to help it grow (intention, attention, attitude, etc.).
- » Be patient.

Monkey mind

Following a mindfulness gathering by the lake with health care professionals, I decided to write a short note about compassion with photographs to commemorate the event. I quickly typed out a narrative. I wanted to say, as healthcare professionals, that we give unselfishly. I wanted to highlight how mindfulness meditation facilitates this. In my haste, however, I scripted the words selfishly and mediation instead, and sent it to attendees. Luckily, my Wise Wife caught this error and brought it to my attention. When we rush, we make mistakes. Our mind is like a monkey that flips from tree to tree, never settling long enough to be present. Autopilot kicks in as we attempt to multitask but this sets us up for failure.

Practice

- » Take time today to simply slow down, unselfishly!
- » Recognize the nature of the monkey mind.

Slow down and enjoy the ride

I was on a shuttle with a group of twenty, heading from Denver airport to the Shambhala Mountain Center, three hours into the mountains at Red Feather Lake. We were all quite eager to get to our final destination, having come from all ends of the continent to be part of a one-week silent mindfulness retreat. Along the way, we approached a railroad track and the gate descended, bringing our bus to an abrupt halt. Then, what appeared to be the longest train in the world emerged at a turtle's pace crawling forward.

On the shuttle, there were sighs of discontent, feelings of frustration, and concern that we would never get there. Just as it looked like the train was passed, it stopped abruptly and then proceeded to reverse, creeping backwards.

This is similar to how our minds work, when we practise meditation. We try to rush our meditation time, just to get it over with. We want to arrive to our destination of wakefulness quickly, with no delay. Our eagerness, however, often slows us down, and gives us no choice but to return to the breath and start all over again. This takes patience and perseverance. This is not a failure.

In the end, the train did finally depart and we proceeded. When you go to the practice of meditation, today, slow down and enjoy the ride.

Practice

» Allow for obstacles to your meditation practice to emerge.
» Notice where you feel it in your body when you encounter barriers.
» Learn from them.
» Know that they are common.
» Enjoy the ride.

Timeless space

It was an ensemble of electronic music pulsation, washing machine-like swishing, banging, and drilling. My body cocooned in this container of steel. Swallowing me, it took magnetic resonance imaging (MRI) detailed pictures of the organs and tissues within my body. I lay motionless, not wanting to compromise this long-awaited medical test in any way. Five minutes turned to fifteen, and fifteen to thirty. Like a time capsule, I found myself enveloped in a timeless space where all I could do was to be present. I couldn't do anything about the series of events that had led up to this moment and I couldn't allow my mind to wonder into the "sea of what ifs." It was a quintessential opportunity to be mindful.

Practice

- » It can be very challenging to be still during meditation.
- » It is perfectly fine to move your body gently and quietly if you need to adjust.
- » When possible, shift to other mindfulness practices (walking, yoga, laying, standing, sitting, etc.).
- » Use a pillow, a blanket or additional props to help maintain your posture, especially over longer durations.
- » Short, guided meditations at the beginning of your mindfulness practice might be helpful.
- » Don't give up.

Writers Block

Once a week, I write a mindfulness meditation blog. Writing is usually self-reflective and effortless. Last evening was different. I sat and looked at my iPad, baffled. When I shared with my Wise Wife that I had no clue what to write, she suggested that I write about not knowing what to write. We had traveled on the weekend and a return to work had left me feeling depleted. I needed rest and time for me, and I honoured this requirement. I knew I was on the right path this morning when I jumped out of bed after a good night's rest, and grabbed my pen and paper ready to write.

Practice

- » Sometimes it is just too difficult to meditate.
- » No matter how hard you try, it seems impossible.
- » During these times you may feel agitated and fidgety.
- » Don't force something that doesn't feel right.
- » Come back to it when you are ready.

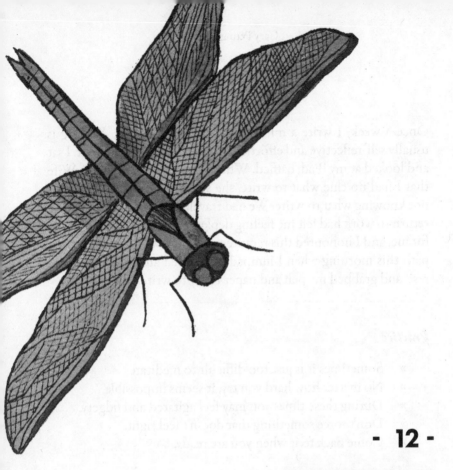

- **12** -

GIFTS BEFORE YOU

One of my mentors, taught me that the practice of mindfulness does not have to be a somber undertaking and we can actually have fun while meditating when we practice with openness, spaciousness, and curiosity. This approach to meditation and to life invites us to be open to discovering the many gifts before us. Sometimes, these gifts come in packages that are not appealing to us at that moment. Sometimes, they come in the pretense of requiring effort, when they only require presence. When we stop and just be, welcoming rather than pushing away, we can enjoy the beauty these gifts bring, and most importantly, have fun and learn through the experience.

For Nate

I will be a new grandfather in the next couple of months. My eldest daughter, Blue Eyes, and son-in-law are expecting their first child. Both of my grandfathers died when I was very young, so sadly, I have no recollection of them nor their influence on my development. I hope I will have beginner's eyes to delight in all that my first grandchild brings. I hope I will be patient and enjoy each moment without fast-forwarding to the next. I hope I will trust that this new little human being will have the inner resources to live in equanimity, enjoying all life brings, the pleasant, neutral, and the unpleasant. I hope, one day, I can share with this child mindfulness practice to see clearly and enjoy the beauty of our world as a playful explorer. I hope I can just be with this grandchild, enjoying each moment and open to learning more from them about mindfulness than any book or course could ever teach me.

Practice

- » Practise true presence with the children in your life (put away your electronic devices).
- » Look into their eyes...really look.
- » Be open to all they have to teach us as mindfulness mentors.

Gifts come from unexpected places

I was tired. I walked to the waiting reception area three times to retrieve my patient to no avail. Then a receptionist called to advise my patient would be forty minutes late but assured me they were on their way. By this time, I was frustrated. I knew this meant a late lunch or no lunch. I knew there would be a delayed cascading effect to my work schedule, reflective of how my day would unfold.

Finally, I received a call, the patient had arrived. The clock was ticking. Once again, I walked to the waiting room and called out the patient's name. Then, from the corner of my eye, emerged a patient of profound radiance, gifted with eyes that spoke and a smile that was infectious. The patient thanked me profusely and then told their story. It was a tale of perseverance, betrayal, and great sadness. My patient was in much pain, but managed to hold on to hope and positivity. As the clock ticked beyond noon, I gently waved my lunch goodbye and relaxed in this gift called "presence." Gifts come from unexpected places. We just need to be open to them, put our agenda aside, and trust.

Practice

» Be open to the gifts before you, even the ones that arrive inconveniently.

Happy spiritually, artistically, and scholastically

Last night, as I typed away on my iPad, my wife asked me what my most favourite gift has been over the past year. This year marked the completion of my Masters in Social Work degree. My family celebrated my achievement with many gifts. They gave me a leather bag, a painting, a concrete Buddha statue for my garden and a new iPad. So, the answer to my wife's question posed a bit of a quandary to me. After a moment of silence, I responded, "Well, the leather bag makes me happy tactilely, the Buddha statue makes me happy spiritually, the painting makes me happy artistically, and the iPad makes me happy scholastically."

Practice

» Take a moment to pause. Breathe.
» Reflect on the gifts that surround you.
» Appreciate the unique qualities that each brings.
» Give gratitude.

The awakened one

It had been one of those days. Several patients back to back, forfeited breaks, fatigue and wanting to seriously examine other career options. Last appointment of the day, with limited attentiveness and empathy left. In saunters a patient for assessment. Longstanding illness, multiple complications, disease weariness, high motivation for change. Unwavering presence, intimacy, and ironically sporting a t-shirt with a picture of a Buddha on it. The word Buddha means "Awakened One," one who is awakened to actuality, who understands true nature of the mind, the world, and all sentient beings. This late afternoon arrival made me smile from within, thankful for this gentle invitation to wake up to all gifts before me.

Practice

» Take a moment to pause and come to stillness.
» Breathe.
» Celebrate your buddha nature (enlightenment).
» Acknowledge that this one simple action can change how you see the world.
» Smile.

Through the clouds

As circumstance would have it, I was traveling home on an airplane. I wanted an aisle seat, but I ended up buckled against the outer steal wall of this metal container, adjacent to a window. Tired, I drifted in and out of consciousness, but was awakened to the warmth of sunshine shining on my contorted torso and overhead the announcement of the pilot preparing us for landing. I gazed out of the window, noticing the bed of clouds beneath. As we descended more deeply, cutting through the clouds, I noticed the emergence of the landscape dotted with houses, streams, lakes, and trees revealing themselves to me. In that moment, it dawned on me, this was what mindful awareness was all about. It's all there within us and right in front of us, beneath the layers of our consciousness waiting to be discovered. Mindfulness provides us with a window seat from which to truly see.

Practice

» Try to see the less than obvious during your day.
» Be a curious observer.
» Look deeply.

The body

Our bodies are remarkable containers that invite us to notice. There is so much of this living breathing organism that we frequently take for granted – disinterested, unappreciative. When mind and body are working together in unison, we are able to pay attention and this results in wiser action. It is often only when a piece of this container comes at risk that we even bother to learn about its function, its importance, and what it might be like to live without it, compromised. Be grateful for this body, listen to it with earnest attention and welcome its many changes. It is a gift.

Practice

» Find a quiet space where you can be alone with your body.
» Scan its parts. Celebrate its majesty. Awe in its complexity.

Batman

I hopped on my bike in a mad dash at the end of a hectic workday. Like Batman donning the batmobile, I straddled the seat, threw on my pack sack, slung my jacket like a cape over my shoulder, fastened my helmet, and fearlessly journeyed home, dodging traffic and all that got in my way. I peddled vigorously, slowing just enough to notice muted shades of brown, black and rust coloured rock, distant lakes, and white birch tree lines. This space from work to home allows me time to transition and to let go of the day. It distances me from the work stressors of the day and provides opportunity for replenishment. It invites me to bask in the moment and ride hands free.

Practice

» Take some time at the end of your workday to transition.
» This means finding some space between what was and what will be.
» Know that you have the inner resources required for whatever Gotham has in store.

Simplicity

We knelt down and peaked through the fly into the lime green three-man tent to see two sleeping bags, two blow up mattresses and a flashlight. Such simplicity. Such happiness. A place of calm. We have complicated so much of our lives. A perpetual state of hyperarousal has become our new norm. We worry often needlessly and fail to appreciate the simplicity of the moment. Mindfulness is a kind reminder of this gift.

Practice

> » Take some time to reacquaint yourself with nature.
> » This might be through a hike, camping excursion or gentle walk.
> » Use all of your senses. Enjoy the simplicity of being with nature and all of its healing qualities.

The sweet sound of her voice

We are fortunate to have Anna-Maria help us with household tasks. She usually arrives to our front door at the crack of dawn with her slippers in hand and a bright smile on her face. She comments on the weather. We hang her coat and off she heads on a mission to clean our house from top to bottom. Within moments of her arrival until she departs, we hear the wash buckets being filled, the vacuum cleaner humming, and amongst this, cleansing bedlam emerges the sweet sound of her voice. Anna-Maria sings from the top of her lungs as she waves her feathered duster and wipes any surface that she can get her hands on. My daughters typically roll their eyes as her voice predictably escalates. My Wise Wife refers to her as having good karma. Anna-Maria is genuine, humble, and delightful. We joke that we would hire her just to visit and sing. We secretly envy her "Joie de vivre".

Practice

> » Take a few moments today to do some housecleaning of your own.
> » Remove the debris that weighs you down. Clear out the negativity that no longer serves you.
> » Most importantly, sing from the top of your lungs with full awareness.

Swans everywhere

While walking along an urban corridor, I arrive at an expansive view of a waterway that stretches to a nearby distant lake. I am able to see beaver dams, cattails, and concrete silhouettes of buildings around the periphery. I notice something quite majestic amongst the backdrop. Two snow white trumpeter swans gliding gracefully down the corridor. I stop and watch in awe, an unexpected gift at the end of a busy workday, that I would have missed had I not stopped to look. Enjoy the majesty of the moment. There are swans everywhere, externally and internally, just waiting to be seen.

Practice

> » In your hurriedness, open your eyes.
> » Look for majesty among concrete, just waiting to be discovered.

My mindfulness mentor

I saw her. She sat there stoic, silent, and with calm presence. She appeared to be an observer, gazing with curiosity and wisdom. Her silhouette was majestically outlined by the sunrise. She was a crane, perched on a rock outcropping. For me, it was reassuring to know that she was there and, in that moment, she became my mindfulness mentor.

Practice

» There are many mindfulness mentors out there that have a lot to teach us about the practice if we are receptive.
» Look. Notice. Let them be our revered teachers.

Lost in camouflage

While walking to work I noticed a blue mitt perched gently on the end of a tree branch. I would have passed right by it had I not paused and looked. With the fresh snowfall, it sat there, looking like it had always been part of the scenery. Motionless, beautiful, and lightly dusted in white, it resembled a sculpture. It had a story to tell. Had it once protected a small child's hand from the harsh cold? Was it a past gift from a doting grandparent? Did the person who lost it even realize that it was missing? Like the lost mitt in the tree, we can easily get lost in the camouflage of everyday existence and miss all of what lies in front of us, just waiting to be dusted off and explored with open eyes.

Practice

> » The next time you journey, stop and pause along the way.
> » Look beyond the camouflage. Beneath the obvious to the obscure.
> » Explore what's there with all of your senses.

Aftermath

With the influx of newspaper flyers advertising upcoming Black Friday sales, I found myself purposefully paying attention to the non-colour of white as I walked to work following an intense snowfall. The past few days have been filled with fog, melancholy, and darkness. The peril of the stock market crashing years ago is now marked with much consumerism. There is also an appetite to find and purchase material objects that will bring distraction and immediate gratification. We don't want to sit with the pain. Escaping seems more palatable. Unfortunately, quick fixes are temporary. True happiness cannot be bought. We are most happy when we are fully present in the moment, open to the aftermath of what is to follow.

Practice

> » Be mindful the next time you wish to purchase something.
> » Take a moment to pause and breathe.
> » Ask yourself the question "Do I need this, or is this solely for distraction?"
> » Sit with what it is you are attempting to be distracted from.

Snow storms

I love snow storms. They have a special ability to bring me to the present moment in a unique way. In stillness, if I listen carefully, I can hear the subtle sound of snowflakes falling from the sky gently colliding with my nylon jacket. I can stick my tongue out and mindfully taste each snowflake delicacy. I can walk mindfully as I shovel the driveway zigzagging back and forth with spaciousness and curiosity, not destination driven. I can feel my feet caressing the earth with each and every footstep, trailblazing through fresh snow with beginner's eyes.

Practice

- » Walking meditation is a formal mindfulness practice.
- » To begin, place your hands, with one cradling the other, resting comfortably on your belly.
- » Walk at a natural pace, either back and forth, or in a circular pattern. This is not about getting somewhere. It's more about cultivating awareness.
- » Pay attention to the lifting and falling of your feet with each and every step.
- » Notice movement in your legs and the rest of your body.
- » Your object of awareness is the sensation of walking.
- » If your mind wanders, gently guide it back to the sensation of walking.
- » It is common to feel that you may lose your balance and fall over when walking mindfully. Don't be concerned about this if it happens.
- » At any time, you may stop, pause, and notice, using all of your senses (sounds, sights, scents, sensations, etc.).
- » You are fully aware, and walking.

Steps

On my right wrist, I wear an exercise tracking device. This is an electronic gadget that calculates the number of steps that I take each day. It was a gift that I have chosen to wear. It unobtrusively gathers data on my every move, the quality of my sleep, my heartrate, and the routes that I navigate. Like my autonomic nervous system that functions largely unconsciously and regulates bodily functions such as the heart rate, digestion, and respiratory rate, this device does all of this background work while allowing me the gift of being fully present.

Practice

- » Stop and take a moment to notice how your body works to keep you alive without you even knowing it.
- » Pay attention to your respiration.
- » Notice your heartbeat.
- » Feel your blood flow.
- » Be grateful for this important background work that often goes unnoticed.

The quiet observer

We settled in. It was a Friday evening and we decided to kick off the weekend by going for dinner at our favourite pizza place. The restaurant was busy. I sat with my family happy to be there, catching up on the week's events. It was then that, out of the corner of my eye, I caught a glimpse of a father and son sitting across from us. They were also with family. The father extended his arm and began to gently caress the back of his son's neck. He massaged it subtly in a kind and loving manner. As an onlooker, I could tell how much he loved this boy. This father beamed in his son's presence. It was so comforting to quietly observe.

Practice

» Be a quiet observer.
» Catch a glimpse of what surrounds you.
» Mindfulness can be a window to uncharted beauty.

Test of my patience

My Wise Wife has just purchased a new coffee pot. It is glass and looks like an hourglass in design. One inserts a paper cone filter, fills the filter with ground coffee, and then pours boiled water over the ground coffee beans while the liquid drips to eventually produce three lovely cups of bold tasting coffee. The process is extremely slow, the drip minuscule. This is a test of my patience when there is an automatic coffee maker, disconnected and tucked at the back of the cupboard. The whole process takes about fifteen minutes. Sometimes, I find it painful. It prevents me from other opportunities to relax before the daily routine gets started. I am coming to realize, however, that this is a gift – a time to be in the moment, attentive with curiosity, and sometimes even humour.

Practice

» Pause.
» Breathe.
» Slow down and enjoy the process.

"I didn't hear a word of her story, did you?"

Finally, some reprieve at lunch from the jackhammers and construction above my office, and back to back meetings. The sound of fans, microwave ovens, and chatter filled the lunchroom.

Across from me sat a soft-spoken colleague who began to tell me a story. Her eyebrows lifted with intonation and her lips moved, but I could not hear a word she was saying. My first instinct was to consider that my hearing was deteriorating and I needed to see an audiologist. I nodded and smiled politely trying to be respectful of her story telling, but I was totally perplexed about what she was trying to convey. When the colleague finished her story another co-worker adjacent, nudged me and whispered "Gary, I didn't hear a word of her story, did you?"

Practice

» Take time today to be truly present with someone.
» Mindfully listen to what the other is saying – paying attention to the words spoken, the way they are conveyed, body language, and meaning of it all.
» Mindful communication and mindful listening are a high form of respecting and gifting another.

- 13 -

BEGINNER'S EYES

If you watch a child at play, you may marvel at their ability to look at the world with beginner's eyes. As we grow older our way of seeing becomes distorted. Our ability to see clearly may be influenced by biases and beliefs, past events, and societal expectations, causing us to see things radically different than what they are. Misperception heightens fear. Fear narrows our ability to think rationally and this causes us to be reactive, completely contrary to being emotionally intelligent. This is an invitation to see for the first time, like a child does, with inquisitiveness and fluidity.

A premonition of a new journey

We have construction occurring above the clinic where I work. It has not been uncommon to hear the sound of drills, sledgehammers, and jackhammers. We have now been advised that we must relocate our offices temporarily to a quieter area in the building. In preparation for the move, I slide the large grey shredding container into my office and I begin to sort through years of accumulation. As a pack rat, I have kept remnants of projects passed and of those that have never materialized. I have found outdated journals and articles that I had kept just in case. This purging is liberating. A segue to a simpler way of being. A divesting of no longer needed items. A relinquishment of burden and a reminder of our intrinsic simplicity and basic goodness. A passageway. A premonition of a new journey.

Practice

> » The act of decluttering, invites you to notice.
> » Pause, breathe, and see.
> » Reflect...Are the objects that you are keeping helpful? Are they making you happy?
> » Is it time to let them go?

A welcomed interruption

A patient's child dashed out in the hallway adjacent to my office door. He was about three years old with beautiful jet back hair and a magical smile. As he ran by, he inquisitively paused and looked in at me, waiting for a response. I looked back and smiled with gratitude for this welcomed interruption. He was curious and looked so innocent. I envied his ability to look with open eyes, not yet influenced by fixed notions, judgment, and self-doubt.

Practice

» If your day is interrupted by a visitor, pause and look with beginners eyes.
» Welcome them as a gift.
» Learn from their curiosity.
» Look into their eyes and let them know that you are present.
» Thich Nhat Hanh reminds us that there is no greater gift to your beloved than the gift of presence.

Viewing the world with unfaltering inquisitiveness

I brought my youngest daughter, Brown Eyes, to our local bus terminal. As we waited for her bus to arrive, we sat, chatted, and 'people watched.' There were nieces making sure that their aunts were fine, university students eager to get home, and lovers reluctantly saying goodbye.

But then we focused on a little boy, no more than two years old, who entered the building with his parents. Curiously, he reached out to look at and touch anything before him. He spotted the arcade game that simulated driving by gripping the toy steering wheel. He touched each and every floor tile. He touched every button he could get his hands on. He said hello and smiled at anyone that would give him a glimpse of acknowledgment. He playfully greeted us. I quietly admired this child's freedom in viewing the world with unfaltering inquisitiveness. Mindfulness brings out the child in all of us.

Practice

- » Take a few moments today to view your world with a child's curiosity.
- » Use all of your senses.

Beauty in a waiting room

I sat there in the hospital laboratory waiting for my number to be called. Sitting directly across from me was a woman with a lovely smile. There was no mobile phone in hand – she was fully present and wanting to engage in conversation. We exchanged niceties about the weather. Registering at the desk was a young couple. She was very pregnant and had an overnight bag, likely checking in to deliver a new baby. An anxious soon to be father hovered over her. An older woman with beautiful piercing blue eyes in a wheelchair, dropped her cane on the floor, and struggled to pick it up. I swooped to her rescue. Another woman teased her husband. An older man in fine clothing sat quietly. I wonder what he was thinking. I have sat in many medical waiting rooms through the years but I have not noticed such beauty in a waiting room before. I don't know why. Maybe I was ready to look with open eyes and understand that I was not alone.

Practice

» Stop to observe the beauty that surrounds you, even in unexpected places.

It's time to laugh and frolic once again

From the kitchen window, I could hear the unfamiliar sound of children's laughter and frolicking. We live in a neighbourhood that has matured. Older neighbours have moved away, slowly being replaced by young new families. It is typically very quiet on the street so the sound of children this late in the evening is welcome, yet foreign. As children, we delight in everything. We see things with freshness. As we grow older, we often become more guarded in our beliefs and our behaviours. This rigidity causes us to miss out on the awe of life. Mindfulness reminds us to wake up. It fosters connection and refuels our zest for living. Mindfulness invites us to laugh and frolic once again.

Practice

» Open a window.
» Listen with full presence.
» Enjoy.

The journey

I remember one cold winter day, years ago, standing in a busy hospital entrance corridor, waiting for my bus to arrive. Between the opening of doors, the constant hum of passersby and the whoosh of freezing air that would gush in each time the door opened, a friend from my university days walked in.

Dressed in a dark trench coat and sporting a leather briefcase, he was impressive to me as someone who turned his education into a great job as a hospital social worker. As time would have it, I was successful in obtaining employment at the hospital as well. I was assigned to a geriatric unit, general medicine, coronary care, and surgery. I was busy. I made mistakes and became a human sponge, soaking up new experiences, medical jargon, the organization's dynamics. I felt so grateful to be exposed to the sanctity of the human condition. I loved everything about working in the hospital. The aged smell of cleansers, floor wax layers, and clean linens, I loved what I did and could not get enough of it.

Practice

- » Pause and go to the breath.
- » Take a moment today to reflect on the first days of a job.
- » Close your eyes and remember how you felt.
- » What compelled you to this work in the first place?
- » Has anything changed?
- » If it has wavered, what can you do to find joy in this work once again?
- » Be kind to self and proceed with awareness, confidence, and hope.

Fog

It's been one week since I left my day job at the hospital. The sun still comes up, even against the dark sky of November. I still feel relevant, perhaps even in a deeper, more spiritual way. I have noticed children on bicycles in my neighbourhood, who are typically not around when I have arrived home after five. I have even been privy to the neighbourhood gossip that I had not been aware of in my work-mode autopilot existence. In some ways, I feel like I have been in a fog. A return to stillness has afforded an opportunity to see, hear and feel more clearly.

Practice

» Don't let work consume you.
» There is so much more beyond the walls of your workplace.
» Breathe, pause, open your eyes to it.
» Lift the fog.

More forgiveness

While at department planning meeting, we examined the organizations new strategic plan and expectations from key stakeholders. One of the points that required discussion and clarification was "more forgiveness, less policing." These words jumped out from the white board like a neon sign. The facilitators asked the staff what this meant. I fessed up that I was the culprit who suggested it. I clarified that my intention with this point was to highlight the patient's requirement for staff nonjudgment. In my work, we can get sidelined with treatment adherence and frequent interrogation. I suggested that we adapt a more compassionate approach to patient care, one that strives to help the patient understand the benefits and consequences of their actions, and that gives them "some latitude as human beings." My supervisor has asked me to try to come up with a visual to help staff be aware of this need in their frontline practice. I will suggest a visual of putting on a new lens. A new lens offers opportunity to see with less bias and restriction. It offers flexibility and a kinder way of being. The new lens will be sharpened by the practice of mindfulness. I really cannot think of a more appropriate tool that will foster compassion.

Practice

» Take a moment to breathe and reflect.
» Am I quick to judge?
» Can I be self-righteous and rigid in my thinking?
» Does this serve me or limit me?
» Can I be more open and compassionate?

The children instinctually see it

I always witness the first snowfall as an opportunity for a new beginning. To many, it signifies a change from darkness to lightness, from gloominess to hope. It offers a "new lens" from which to view our world. The children instinctually see it, but as adults, we simply need to open up our eyes to it. I noticed a young boy, angelic looking, simply standing with his arms extended, catching snowflakes and taking the time to truly look at and taste each one of them. He embraced them. He observed each snowflake, their texture, their imperfections, and their beauty.

Practice

- » Look for new beginnings.
- » Breathe. Notice. Play.

Inquisitiveness

As I entered the pathway at the end of a long run, I noticed a little girl about the age of three. She had rosy cheeks, was bundled up in warm clothing, and took delight in the dog that had harnessed her attention. Her older brother and her mother were directly behind her with watchful eyes. She captured the essence of being able to look at the world with fascination. She appeared to appreciate what was in front of her. She seemed to delight in this inquisitiveness.

Practice

- » Be inquisitive.
- » Appreciate all that is right in front of you.
- » Delight in it all.

To another day

Quietness envelopes the clinic where I work. The sound of the custodian's mop rattles with each sway. Co-workers closing doors, Microsoft Office software shutdown jingle, and filing cabinets closing and locking. The day comes and goes. All is well. To another day.

Practice

- » At the end of your workday, resist the urge to just leave.
- » Linger for a couple of moments quietly, just listening to the sounds.
- » Put to rest this day and prepare to welcome a new day with open eyes.

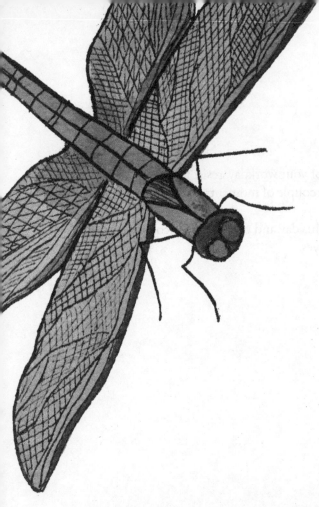

OPPORTUNITIES THAT HELP US TO GROW

When we stop learning, we risk becoming complacent. The practice of mindfulness encourages us to be creative and welcome all opportunities for growth. We learn to think outside of the box rather than to cling to what is comfortable. Growth is non-linier. It can be both frightening and exciting at the same time. Some teachers are obvious while others are less apparent. Mindfulness helps us to be aware of the less obvious teachers in our life and welcome all. This valuable lesson requires self-compassion and trust.

Missed opportunities

"Hey mom and dad, how about joining us in a yurt this weekend?" said Blue Eyes. "We will have fun, play board games, hike, and have good food!" A yurt is a type of round tent with a wooden floor and frame, uninsulated but equipped with a heater, bunk beds, and a table. We would go yurting at Killarney Provincial Park. It has been -25 Celsius here, so the invitation sounded interesting but not terribly captivating. It would have been so much easier to just stay home, nice and warm, clinging to predictability and warmth. But this would have been a missed opportunity as this was an invitation to try something different. Turns out it was the best weekend we have had in a long time. Lots of adventures, wine and wonderful time together, so often it is easy to do what is habitual. Sometimes, we need to move beyond our comfort zone to appreciate what we have been missing. The same can be applied to our work and homelife. We can coast, just getting by, or we can explore new opportunities that might revive us and refuel our zest for living.

Practice

>> Pause, be still, reflect.
>> Too comfortable in your work, your relationships, your being?
>> Challenge yourself by moving beyond your comfort zone.
>> Treat these new opportunities as an adventure.
>> Be a playful explorer.
>> Do so with full awareness and openness.
>> Celebrate growth.

The real world awaits

We sat in a circle and delivered our presentation. My Wise Wife and I were asked to speak to a fourth-year university social work class on the topic of mindfulness and resilience. These students looked so fresh and inexperienced. At the end of the presentation, they were able to accurately summarize, but I am not convinced they actually understood the real message being delivered. How could they at this point in their career? Being a social worker is emotionally demanding. You never know what will happen when each client walks in through your door and begins to tell their story. The essence of their pain and suffering. The emotional ups and downs. The journey that you walk together, even when you would rather just curl up and take refuge. The real world awaits them, just as it had opened its arms to us. I hope it is kind to them.

Practice

> »   Don't underestimate the value of your shared wisdom.

Layers

I began my post-secondary schooling determined to be an English teacher. Into my first year of studies, I realized my interest was geography. I switched my major and completed an honours degree in this new-found discipline.

The next layer was one of awakening to the reality that, in the mid 1980's, the employment options for new geography graduates were few. My Wise Wife was a social worker and I found myself very interested in "her" discipline, constantly clipping newspaper articles that dealt with social issues. I returned to school and completed an Honours Bachelor of Social Work degree with a vision to understanding people so I could eventually work in urban planning and appreciate the population for whom I would be designing cityscapes.

The next layer was one of innocence lost. I had lived a rather sheltered life, growing up in a small steel town. Exposure to the world of welfare and child protection introduced me to suffering in the world. This was followed by a layer of entry into medical social work. I loved this work. I was proud and eager to make a difference. Employment as a nephrology social worker became available and this became a layer of rapid growth, knowledge, and professional connection.

The next layer was one of critical thinking and self-confidence as I returned to university to complete my Master of Social Work degree. My fascination with mind-body medicine awakened my senses and proved to be a layer of enhanced therapeutic presence, compassion, and non- judgment, as I pursued qualification to teach mindfulness. The next layer was to explore the world of diabetes care, wanting to make a difference for those suffering from chronic disease. Leading me to another layer of helping those who help others, healthcare professionals. I continue to acquire more layers.

Practice

» Take some time to reflect on your professional growth and all of the layers that shape your life.

She taught me

I vividly remember being called to this patient's bedside. She was a well accomplished woman of strength and candour. She had taught many students as a respected teacher in the community as well as being instrumental in changing the imbalance of power for women as a strong feminist advocate. She was a mother and a partner. At any other time in her life, I may have shuddered upon meeting her, but today was different.

She was emotionally fragile. She wept inconsolably. Her body lay limp. She was in pain and just wanted to give up. I sat beside her and I held her hand. I didn't have much to say. I was simply there with her. She did not wish to be fixed. She just wanted to be heard. Seconds turned to minutes and minutes to hours, and as years passed by, I spent much time just being with this brave woman. Passerby's on the unit would witness this and make comments to me like "you're different than the other staff" in a curious way.

Truth be told, she was still teaching even in this state of profound loss. She taught me how to be compassionate and present.

Practice

» Don't let your perceptions or interpretations of others stop you from being present and kind.
» Letting someone know that you are there for them is one of the kindest gifts that you can give.
» This is one of life's most valuable lessons.

In good hands

While waiting to see my athletic therapist, I am told by the receptionist, she has been delayed due to being a guest lecturer at the School of Medicine. This information sits well with me. My personal preconceptions allow for it to influence my subjective opinion of her, and whether right or wrong, it seems to validate her credibility in my eyes. Metaphorically, it helps me to feel that I am placing my body "in good hands." When we share our knowledge with others, they grow. When they grow, we grow. When we grow, it shows.

Practice

» Bring to mind professional caregivers or service providers who serve you.
» As you reflect on their presence and service, notice what resonates in the body.

Enriching our "Soles"

As I was preparing to attend an out-of-town educational conference, I went through the ritual of packing my suitcase, usually filled with too many clothes to possibly wear. This also entailed an examination of appropriate footwear, running shoes for those early morning adventures, sandals to slip into at the end of the day, and brown leather dress shoes to wear during the conference. I thought it was fitting that these tattered leather oxfords receive a new coat of shoe polish. I dug out the shoe polishing basket, grabbed an old pair of wool socks, and mindfully applied the umbra brown cream to the thirsty membranes. I reminisced about polishing my father's oxfords every Friday evening when he and my mother would get dressed up to go dancing at the Union Hall. I marveled at the magic of transforming worn shoes into shining vessels that would carry me off with new confidence. New learning opportunities are similar to a new coat of polish. We are immersed in new knowledge that satisfies our thirst and makes it possible for us to dance again. These experiences transform us and feed our "soles."

Practice

- » Embrace new learning opportunities as they present.
- » Touch, feel, and breathe them with full presence.
- » Allow them to quench your thirst.

Finding calm

We lined up preparing to navigate through airport security. The security guard ordered that we get out our passports and move forward. He belted this out in an unfriendly manner, reminiscent of the speaker that blurts out names in hospital waiting rooms. The closer we stepped towards the scanners the more heightened our distress, once again, reminiscent of what our patients endure anticipating medical tests.

Then, to our surprise, we suddenly heard the sound of a security guard singing. He did not reprimand us nor make us feel less than human. He sang a Bob Marley tune, with lyrics suggesting we smile, move forward and have a lovely day. Onlookers caught unprepared stopped suddenly to try to make sense of this music. Smiles lit up previously bewildered faces. This man dared to be different.

This reminded me of a time walking past a hospital waiting room. It appeared busy, noisy, and unfriendly. As a hospital staff, I would have typically just continued on, but for some reason, I stopped.

I sat down and asked if patients would like to participate in a mindfulness awareness of breath formal practice. With curiosity, they agreed. Stress levels diminished and patients headed to their treatment with smiles. Just like the airport security guard, I took a chance and used unconventional action as a unique opportunity. Together, we found calm.

Practice

» When challenging situations arise, be open.
» Try to look at them with open eyes.
» Treat them as unique opportunities... unconventional teachers.
» Learn from their wisdom.

Beyond my comfort zone

There's a reason why I became a social worker. I am not good in math nor am I mechanically inclined. For me, the occupation of social work has been a good fit. The work is challenging but very rewarding. As a seasoned professional, my work is comfortable, like a pair of well broken-in leather shoes.

Every so often, there is an occurrence that reinforces my career path decision. The most recent reminder was the discovery of a flat tire on my car, parked in the driveway.

I was tired, mosquitos ravenous. I simply wanted to pretend it wasn't there. Circumstances beyond my control rattled me. Together with my daughter's boyfriend, we dug out the own-er's manual, located the jack and spare tire, and repaired the flat. Mindfulness pushes us out of comfort and defines scopes of prac-tice. It helps us to deal with unexpected circumstances without being overwhelmed. This push beyond our comfort zone helps us to learn.

Practice

» Uncomfortable situations arise, often with no owner's manual to guide us through them.
» Welcome each flat tire in your life as an opportunity to learn, even when you are feeling deflated.

Lessons learned

When my father-in-law passed, my family and I took our place at the funeral home visitation. We stood at the entrance way like soldiers greeting all who arrived. It was like being on the dance floor and balcony at the same time. This is so much of what mindfulness is all about, being both a participant and an observer – the dance floor being the conversation, the interchange, the dialogue, and the balcony being a bird's eye view of visitors arriving and departing. Some inconsolable. Some in shock. Some puzzled by the mystery of life and death, simply trying to make sense of it all. For me, a profound teachable experience with valuable lessons.

Practice

» We all create storylines and don't like amendment without warning.
» We all suffer and are undeniably connected at a much deeper level than one can explain.
» Taking time to look in a person's eyes can tell you much

more than the utterance of words.
» We only have this moment.
» Seize it my friends!

The ace

I noticed a single playing card lying on the pavement. As I looked closer, I realized that it was the ace of diamonds. I initially continued walking, but then remembered the ace is ranked as the highest card in its suit in most card games and thought it might bring me good fortune. With this in mind, I turned, picked it up, and slid it in my breast pocket. Life is filled with many teachers, and whether it be the two of clubs or the ace of diamonds, both have lessons to teach us if we choose to listen. We often place a lot of significance on persons and things in our life, based on values and hierarchy. This limits us. Treat each honourably.

Practice

» Notice how you form judgment, often based on assumptions.
» Does doing so always result in good fortune?
» Can you enjoy the full deck of happenings and visitors in your life?

The apple vendor

While at the farmers market, we stumbled upon an apple vendor. He displayed many apple varieties and we eventually settled on the "Honey Crisp" variety. Tucked in the far-right corner of his display, we noticed a jar of apple butter, and as I quickly grabbed it, he mentioned that he had other items for sale. He took out a jar of apple jalapeño jelly, followed by other apple condiments, and we snapped them up. He mentioned that he also had some homemade baking items that might interest us. Out came a fresh apple, strawberry pie, then a homemade pumpkin pie. In the end, he cut us a deal as we loaded up our finds, happy to have found him. Like the apple vendor, we too have the extraordinary ability to draw upon inner resources when we need them most. I like to tell my participants in the mindfulness program they are being prepared to practise mindfulness skillfully by using a full smorgasbord of formal and informal practices to help them be fully aware and to feast in this moment.

Practice

» You have learned a variety of formal mindfulness practices.
» Be self-assured that you can draw upon these resources when you need them.

See clearly

I was on all fours, scrubbing the bottom of the shower stall, when I suddenly felt an abrupt hit to my head. The removable shower head had let go and swung downward, striking me on the back of my head. Firstly, it hurt. It was startling, humorous, and humbling. Later in the day, my last appointment arrived with his head down as he made his way to my office. He shared how he was struggling with his chronic disease regime. When I asked what he needed from the team, he responded, "I need someone to hit me over the head and tell me that if I don't smarten up, I will have serious repercussions."

Sometimes, we all need to pause. This doesn't always come easy for us as we are so driven by our tasks, jobs, roles, and narratives. The analogy of being hit over the head simply signifies the essential requirement of turning inward and taking inventory, paying close attention to our thoughts, emotions, and our body. This helps us to be present, see clearly, and act wisely.

Practice

> » Pause and take inventory.
> » Pay attention to thoughts, emotions, and body sensations.
> » You can only make change when you see clearly first.

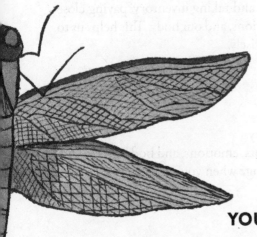

YOUR INNER RESILIENCE

Mindful awareness is innate in all of us. We all have the capacity to bounce back from difficult times with hope and confidence, but this needs to be cultivated through our meditation practice. It doesn't just happen. We need to do the work to reap the benefits, and one benefit is an enhanced ability to be with pleasant, unpleasant and neutral events in our life. Stress is not a bad thing in and of itself. It is how we view the stressful event that defines our ability to deal with it effectively. Exposure to chronic stress over a prolonged time wears us out physically and psychologically. Clinging to what was or pushing away what is only complicates our situation, causing more suffering. When we accept all of which is, we find stability and develop buoyancy to life's challenges that we face daily. We become more resilient and we find equanimity. This gives us great freedom.

Riding with confidence and resilience

In the photograph, he looked confident and self-assured. Brown Eye's boyfriend purchased a brand-new mountain bike and she sent us this image so we could witness his excitement from afar. Many of us may remember getting our first new bike, a vehicle to lift us to new heights and make our dreams seem completely attainable. It gives the freedom of riding fearless, balanced with no hands, navigating the ups and downs of the road before us. Like riding a new bike, the acquisition of full awareness, derived through the practice of mindfulness, helps us to navigate our way through life's twists and turns with calm and balance.

Practice

- » Pause and breathe while in a standing yoga posture.
- » Stretch both arms up and outward.
- » In tree pose, with one foot on the ground firmly planted and the other gently resting on your shin or inner thigh, come to stillness.
- » Pause. Breathe. Smile.
- » Now reverse this pose, inviting the other side to follow.
- » Notice how the body works in unison to help you find balance.

Be hope

He quickly rode past me. As a lone cyclist, he dodged his way through traffic and snow. He fled as quickly as he appeared. As I trudged along, cursing the snow, disliking the winter and loathing the sidewalk snow cleaners, I could feel my lips begin to turn upward, forming a smile with this sighting. As a mindfulness practitioner, I could appreciate the humour of this situation, pleasantness in unpleasantness. It gave me hope. It helped me to realize that we are halfway through this winter season and that there will be more cyclists on the horizon with the emergence of spring.

Practice

> » As you dash through your busy day, take time to periodically check in.
> » Is there pleasantness in unpleasant circumstances?
> » Is there unpleasantness in pleasant circumstances?
> » Be hope.

Trudging

Trudging through slush at the end of the workday, on my way to teach a mindfulness session, I started my journey feeling wornout. As time and distance from work furthered, I began to feel my energy reserves return. The group is diverse, made up of varying ages and life experiences. With the unfolding of this session, a participant shared that mindfulness was helping her to be in the moment, even if the moment was time limited. One participant shared that mindfulness had given them courage to be alone, previously frightening. Another shared that mindfulness was assisting her to understand reactive patterns previously denied. On this day, mindfulness gave me calm, picked me up, shook me off, and set me back on my feet again.

Practice

- » Take a pen and journal.
- » Place them by your night table.
- » Each night before bed, take couple of moments to breathe, pause, and make a journal entry.
- » Write about how mindfulness has helped you to get through the day's challenges and events.
- » The art of writing your thoughts to paper invites personal reflection.
- » Be honest and kind to self.

Life

I have been captivated by the Winter Olympics, watching the daily broadcast with anticipation. The athletes are extraordinary. They fly through the air, tapping into their inner resources, push on in the face of adversity, and dust themselves off to face their fears head-on with curiosity and resolve. They have moments that are quite pleasant or unpleasant, and through it all, they appear to get by and learn in the process. Mindfulness has the ability to cultivate our inner resilience given all that we face. We too can be athletes in this great game that we call Life.

Practice

- » Know that you too have this agility to adapt and bounce back.

Cottage number 8

My Wise Wife and I have thought about purchasing a cottage for years. Then one day, while dropping off our youngest daughter, at summer camp, we saw a sign that enticed us to veer off the highway and explore a cottage resort. When we reached the lake, we were instructed to use the phone nestled away in a metal box near the dock. The resort host headed over to pick us up by boat and tour us around. We fell in love with the resort and we made it our annual cottage retreat. Cottage number 8 became ours.

We enjoyed group campfires and met many interesting people. We savoured Tuesday evening hotdog roasts and the warm home-made chocolate chip cookies that were delivered to our door each time we arrived for our annual stay. This was a magical place where Brown Eyes caught frogs until the wee hours of the morning and figuratively kissed one until she found her handsome prince. This place welcomed Blue Eyes and her kayak following each university year, cradling her in its arms, replenishing her. This was the place where we "empty nested" for the first time and knew that Riesling, good food, books, paints and Scrabble would be our companions through this life passage.

I recently learned the property has been sold to new owners. Everything changes. Mindfulness helps us to be with change and to know that we will be okay. In our hearts, cottage number 8 will always be ours.

Practice

» Think of a time in your life when you struggled to hold onto something or someone dear. In the end, were you able to do this? How did your desire to hold on show up in your thoughts, emotions, and body sensations?

When you finally allowed yourself to let go, did anything change? You may wish to explore this concept even further with some gentle lying down yoga.

» Begin by lying flat on your stomach with your arms stretched up, above your head, and your toes pointing downward.

» Now extend your right arm and your left leg, forward and backward, gently feeling a stretching sensation. Hold this pose for a moment, and then allow both to fall to the ground and release.

» Now repeat this posturing, but this time extending the left arm and right leg, so that both are off the ground. Once again, the invitation is to hold this for a moment and then release. Breathe, rest.

» Now, you are welcomed to lift both arms and legs off the ground at the same time, while lying on your stomach in a superman pose. Arms and legs extended. Feel the stretch. Notice how your body feels while holding this pose. Hold it. Then let go. Notice how the body feels with this action.

» Can you relate this to the hard work of the body in holding on to what was? Are you able to take this concept a step further? Did the release offer you a reduction in suffering? What are you able to learn from this mindfulness practice?

A nice ending

Sudbury is a rocky, urban city previously devastated by severe acid rain from the nickel industry that blackened its natural landscape. The city is located in the heart of the pre-Cambrian shield, which was once an area filled with dense pine forests and rich vegetation. Several NASA astronauts trained in Sudbury in the early 1970's and it became known as a city that had more of a moonscape than a landscape. With the passing of time and an effort to regreen and restore the landscape, Sudbury is now a lush oasis of new growth dotted with over 300 lakes within the city limits. It has replenished from being black and desolate to being green and lush. The rocky hills are now covered with wild blueberries that cling to the acidic soil. This story could have ended differently.

Practice

» Take some time in your busy schedule to rescue your landscape.
» Renewal is vital in helping us to continue to be safe, happy, and healthy.
» Mindfulness helps to cultivate renewal.

I have a whole team behind me

As I ran up the hill, I knew something was not right. My heart wanted me to keep going, but my inner wisdom told me otherwise. I wish I would have listened to my instincts. Injured. Miserable. Upon walking to work today, I passed a young woman with visual impairment who pounds the pavement daily with her seeing eye dog. I passed a park bench with an inscription dedicated to a friend who died suddenly. I had coffee with a work colleague, and together, we told stories that validated the gift of living. Before you knew it, my chiropodist friend was chiseling imperfections on my feet, my nurse practitioner colleague was helping me to obtain a written script, and my physiotherapist friend had squeezed me into their busy schedule. They became my adhoc treatment team. They gave me hope. Mindfulness provides us with qualities of clarity, concentration and equanimity – all important, all part of my inner healing team.

Practice

- » Pause. Breathe.
- » Know that you are safe.
- » Welcome all of your blessings.
- » Appreciate that you are well supported and not alone on your journey.

Back into the full swing

Following a restful summer holiday, we all returned to the full swing of life…school… work…activities. I am reminded of this as I sip my coffee, hoping that it will be a miracle remedy that will awaken me after rumination of the previous day's events and a full schedule to get through today. My Wise Wife reminds me that this is a time of transition that requires gentle navigation and self-care, listening to the wisdom of the body.

Practice

> » There are no quick fixes to times of transition.
> » Notice where your body carries physical tension that may accompany this change.
> » Take a moment to pause and go to a yoga pose referred to as "child's pose."
> » On hands and knees, spread your knees wide apart, extend your hands and arms forward, and sit back, gently lowering your torso between your thighs.
> » Rest with full awareness.

" Hey, Bro...what can I do you for?"

My smartphone has been problematic. There is an authorized dealer in town who can repair it but I fear that the cost may be more than I want to spend, and the service suboptimal. My daughters advised me of a repair outfit in a shady area of town that could do the work and potentially charge less.

I arrived to the gray painted, boarded up door. Directions and operating hours were unclear. Windows were boxed up with some peak holes. As I entered with hesitation, the owner warmly greeted me and sputtered "Hey, Bro...what can I do you for?" He sat by the counter with tools in hand like a gifted surgeon about to embark on an exploration. An ensemble of helpers sat in the backdrop, recalling "smartphone war stories."

In the end, the work was completed in a timely manner with a few more endearing terms directed my way, like "Brother, Big Guy, Dude" and my phone was successfully repaired. Although the environment was dingy, the passion to serve was rich and the work good.

Practice

>   Take a moment to breathe.
>   Take a moment to reflect.
>   Do you feel broken?
>   What is important and what is not in the bigger scope of things?
>   Watch for negativity that may not serve.
>   Drop expectations and judgments.
>   Allow for repair.

No supernatural powers

When in Boston recently, I purchased a brand-new pair of running shoes. They are featured in running magazines as "the next best thing to sliced toast." The manufacturer promotes the shoe as having a bouncy spongy heal that will catapult you to new heights. They are bright red and yellow, and they seem to blend quite nicely these days with the colour of autumn leaves.

I dug them out of the stiff cardboard box, smelled their newness, and looked at them with anticipation as I laced them up to begin my daily exodus. After kilometer five, they felt less extraordinary. My feet began to feel numb and my legs seemed to cramp up. Their lustre dissipated with each step. They were not the miracle shoes I had hoped for. In the end, they turned out to be just new bright red shoes with no special qualities or magical powers.

Mindfulness is not a panacea for all that ails us. With its rise in popularity, there is much hype. It is not a one size fits all and it requires commitment to the practice. Mindfulness is not about achieving nirvana nor is it about escape. Just good old plain awareness – moment by moment with no supernatural powers.

Practice

- » Take time today to meditate.
- » Be realistic with your intentions and don't expect the practice of mindfulness to fix all.
- » Be leery of mindfulness teachers who promise more.

Winter Darkness

For days now, we have endured overcast skies. Dampness oozes into our limbs with heaviness and grey pervades our psyche. We open the blinds in the morning to see the emptiness of colour and we leave work devoid of light. This can be a time of the year that takes a toll on us.

We are already stretched to the limit and this daily game of chance that fluctuates between light and darkness challenges us even further.

Practice

- » Take this opportunity to look for your light within.

- 16 -

GIVING SERVICE

My roots in healthcare have strengthened my understanding of the importance of true presence without judgment. We all need to know that we are cared for. When we feel this caring, we have the potential to achieve more favourable outcomes. It is comforting to know that we have someone who is truly present. Mindfulness helps us to move beyond empathy, which is the ability to put yourself in the other person's shoes, going a step further to compassionate benevolent action. This is life giving rather than depleting. The path is long and complicated. It challenges us daily and can cause us suffering. It is difficult enough without being made to feel less whole. Mindfulness helps us to recognize the basic goodness or sacredness in all persons. It is a great connector that banishes inequality and invites us to walk the path together. This is giving service.

Alive

Stop for a moment in your busy day to listen. For me, those are the sounds of patients and staff immersed in chatter. The crescendo of activity during busy and not so busy times. The sound of motorized wheelchairs, canes and walkers, on route to treatment. The pulse of machines with sporadic interludes of beeps and whistles. Blood pressure cuffs inflating and deflating. The ebb and flow. The inhalation and exhalation of the breath.

Practice

» Listen to the echoes of being alive.
» Being with this breath...and this breath...and this breath.
» Notice how these sounds bring you back to the moment, offering you full presence.

Warmth

I am the first in our home to arrive to the manual coffee maker each morning. I systematically set up the coffee, filter, and coffee cups the night before bed. Upon awakening, I boil the kettle and bathe the coffee grounds with boiling water to complete the brewing process. Once I pour my own cup of java, I swaddle the glass carafe with tea towels and crown it with a tea cozy, tucking it in tightly like a father swaddling a baby in an effort to keep it warm.

I remember so many of my dialysis patients being cold, trembling while on treatment. Some staff complained about their request for more layers to keep warm. I just knew that basic needs had to be met first and that warmth was one of them. I would often arrive to the bedside with warm blankets from the blanket warmer, swaddle the patient, tucking them in with their approval, and then get on with other business. It was such a simple gesture but so appreciated and often a catalyst for the warm conversations that followed. It allowed refuge from the harshness of this intrusive treatment, true presence, and shelter from the cold.

Practice

» Go to a sitting meditation posture.
» Take a blanket and wrap it around your body. Swaddle it.
» Place your hands resting gently on your thighs.
» Find warmth and stability.

Armour

I attended a workshop recently where I had the opportunity to see and hear author and speaker, Joan Halifax. She has written several books on Buddhism and spirituality. Her talk was on the theme of "basic goodness," implying that if we are able to look more deeply, we will find basic goodness innate in all human beings. This notion can be very challenging when working in busy hospital units that are often filled with suffering. Hospital patients generally do not want to be there. Quarters are tight and long periods of time with others can cause conflict. Sometimes, it is difficult to see basic goodness in those patients who are most demanding of our time and energy. We all have persons in our life who demand of us. When we are mindful, we are less reactive and more responsive to their demands. We are also able to see underneath the armour and not be sidetracked by their behaviour.

Practice

> » Today, try to see basic goodness in all, even those who push your limits.
> » Open your heart to it.
> » Touch it. Be with it.

Unspoken

There is an unspoken language between runners. While running adjacent to a busy roadway, I caught the profile of another runner slogging through deep snow on the other side. The sighting typically commands a waving gesture that is usually reciprocated. Though separated by the road, we experience an intrinsic feeling of connection. It sends the message "I know your there." I find comfort in knowing this.

Practice

> » Speak less and listen more.
> » Feel the intimacy of deep connection.
> » Notice the unspoken.
> » How does this resonate in your heart, thoughts, and body?

Map ways

Over the past two weeks, we have been participating in "program mapping" based on the premise that if we map our every action on paper, we will be able to recognize inefficiencies and opportunities.

The nurse proceeds by outlining the tangible tasks that she facilitates with the patient, going through a detailed checklist and one by one striking each task off. A finely tailored recipe. The dietitian outlines their tasks. A potato chip has precisely this amount of fat, carbohydrates, and calories. It is exact. Then it comes to the path of the social worker. I find this more intangible to outline.

How does one define the intimate unfolding that occurs from the moment that you greet the patient as they walk through the door of your office to the rise, smile, and hope in their eyes upon leaving? How does one explain the flood of emotions that erupt during the interview, the cradling of them, taking them apart, and the restructuring of them that occurs in that 90-minute time slot? How does one explain patient presence and the sanctity of true listening? How does one describe the influx of compassion? Maps are meant to guide one safely from one point to another. The destination is set. The difficulty is that with human beings the destination is constantly changing. It is seldom stationary. Just as we arrive, we realize that life circumstances will change, and this necessitates recalibration and more movement. I am a guide. I help my patients to navigate. The path is unclear and painful. This I cannot put into words.

Practice

» Drop into the breath.
» Call to mind the clearly defined roles and responsibilities at your place of work.
» Now call to mind the less obvious, the subtle tasks that you deliver, the ones less apparent, the ones that you find difficult to put into words, the ones more ambiguous.
» Notice how your body responds to both.
» Notice the differerence.

Collaborative magic

I have the opportunity to speak to new dietetic interns about collaborative practice in health care. I know this concept well as a mindfulness practitioner and from my exposure to the nephrology (kidney) world. I remember doing one of my first satellite visits to a hemodialysis unit two hours from my home base with a dietitian colleague. The clinic was old and narrow in both space and ideology. When we entered the clinic, we were made to feel like intruders. Staff had no concept of what our role was nor did they appear to have an interest. Both my colleague and I persevered as we believed in patient-centred quality care. Over time and many subsequent visits, we educated, worked from an evidence-based approach, and eventually gained acceptance for what we uniquely brought to the team. We made a difference systematically interviewing each patient with full presence. This was collaborative practice and it was magical.

Practice

- » Breathe.
- » Bring to mind the key players of your work team.
- » Notice the unique attributes that each person brings.
- » Notice your thoughts, feelings, and body sensations as you call to mind each person.
- » Recognize that, just like you, they want to be happy, healthy, and fulfilled in their work. They too want to make a difference.
- » Now set an intention to go forward making a conscious effort to work together.
- » This means no egos, no judgement, and no blaming.

Authenticity

I have been ironing my shirts for work for thirty-three years. I have many shirts to select from, but in simpler times, I had two button down collar shirts that needed to be washed and pressed multiple times a week. As a new graduate, I was taught the importance of professional attire by a social work professor, a force to be reckoned with. Shirts were to be pressed, and I was taught to dress professionally in attire to facilitate comfort and encourage connection. Connection, however, is more than about what we wear. It is fostered by dropping one-upmanship and being on the same playing field. It is about our presence and our actions, our nuances and our judgments. Mindfulness fosters authenticity and dropping pretenses. Anything less will be realized.

Practice

> »   Breathe.
> »   Call to mind the uniforms, roles, and storylines that you have adapted in your place of work.
> »   Reflect. Have you become too comfortable?
> »   Can you be open to moving forward in a new way.
> »   Notice how it feels to think about this change.
> »   Can you move beyond familiar to unfamiliar?

"Hello, Dr. Gary!"

The waiting room was full. Lots of noise, many sighs, and much impatience. I approached and scanned as I called out one of those one syllable names. The room quieted, the noise settled, and my patient seemed nowhere to be found. Then I heard it. "Hello, Dr.

Gary!"

I have a new patient no taller than three feet and who is just four years old. Immersed in the medical system just weeks ago, this patient has come to the conclusion that all members of the interdisciplinary team are physicians. This is not the first time I have heard this child call me doctor. In this child's eyes, there are no hierarchies. Our roles are equally important in the provision of service. No captains, just sailors in this sea of suffering.

Practice

» Take a moment to mindfully reflect on the unique contributions that each member of your personal or professional team brings.
» Celebrate all.

An "ankle biter" and a nocturnal cat!

My eldest daughter, Blue Eyes, has left the nest. She and a friend share a loft in town and this comes with a little dog we initially thought might be an "ankle biter" named Bijou and a nocturnal cat. She has developed an affection for Bijou; however, she and the cat have an understood displeasure for each other. She has not experienced any problems with this feline, but she feels that they simply do not appreciate each other's attributes.

We are always faced with unique personalities. Although we may mutually respect each other, we sometimes have a simple intolerance for the attributes that make us distinctive. Our words and our body language may not be in sync, and like the cat in my daughter's apartment, the people that we interact with can sense our judgment. The practice of mindfulness can assist us in dropping our biases and finding the good in one another.

Practice

> » Breathe. Take a moment to reflect.
> » Are there people in your life who you find difficult to be with?
> » Can they sense your judgment?
> » Are your behaviours contributing to this challenge?
> » Be kind to self and to others and try to see beyond bias.

Out of my comfort zone

In the wee hours of the morning, I began my four-hour journey to Toronto for a medical test. Darkness followed me for the first hundred kilometers, giving way to sunrise that illuminated the backdrop of rocks, lakes, and pine silhouettes. I sipped my coffee to stay awake and mindfully kept my eyes peeled to the side of the highway for any wandering wildlife. When I arrived to the hospital, the waiting area overflowed and conversations lingered. I waited for two hours, had the test, and hopped back into my car for another four hour drive home. I felt out of my comfort zone in the large metropolitan hospital. Finally arriving home felt good. When we give service rather than simply go through the motions, we facilitate safe journey. This approach can only be realized when we are fully awake and have experienced being out of our comfort zone. It is difficult to know suffering until we have suffered.

Practice

> » Push beyond your comfort zone.
> » Allow for the breath to ground you and offer you safety if this gets too uncomfortable.

Good karma

There's a little restaurant off the beaten path we like to frequent. It is nothing fancy but the owner, who is the cook, cashier, and waiter, provides excellent service in an atmosphere that my Wise Wife refers to as good karma. You are warmly greeted, the food is mindfully prepared, and he is happy to meet your needs as best he can with courtesy, warmth, and an indescribable gentleness. The food is delicious. You want to tip him and thank him for his service. It is not a burden to do this. You just want to. Mindfulness encourages us to realize how our actions influence how others will react to us. This lays the foundation for good karma.

Practice

> » Notice how your actions contribute to reactions.
> » Remember that karma is about cause and effect.
> » When you honour and nurture, it comes back in a positive way.

The "Floss Bully"

I walked into my dental office for a regular cleaning only to find out I had been assigned a dental hygienist known as the Floss

Bully. She greeted me at the door and my heart sank as I knew I would be scrutinized for unsatisfactory daily mouth care. I do floss regularly but the Floss Bully has previously reprimanded me for improper technique. She advised that the gum measurer was recording unprecedented recesses and my flossing was substandard. With my mouth open and her instruments chiseling at my teeth, she ranted on excessively about her child who had been on the school basketball team but was confined to the bench as the coach favoured other players. As I lay there helplessly, she used the analogy that I was favouring my top molars but was remiss in caring for the bottom teeth. Her voice increased as she told me to visualize that the bottom teeth were the ones not being included in the game. She dared me to think of one of them as her child. When we are mindful, we come to recognize the unique attributes of all. We view all that we serve as whole and we come to celebrate their sacredness. We are kind and inclusive rather than unkind and divisive. We come to recognize that we are all key players, more alike than not.

Practice

> » Recognize the wholeness of all that you serve.
> » Make sure to help them to feel included in the game.

Mediocrity vs extraordinary

"We're having surf and turf tonight," said my daughter, Blue Eyes. When we arrived, the grill was sizzling, the table was set, and the candles were lit. Our new son-in-law darted in and out of the house, tending to the shrimp, salmon, and steak with precision and navigation as we all anticipated the feast. But the crown that defined the meal was a homemade steak sauce comprised of coffee, sriracha hot sauce, and Dijon mustard. This carefully executed addition catapulted the meal from being wonderful to being extraordinary.

In our work, we may go through the motions of simply offering mediocre service without even being aware. This might include multitasking – getting much done, but not much done well. When we pay attention to what we are doing in our work with full presence, our service excels, we error less, we enjoy our work more, and we are more creative and productive. This catapults us to extraordinary workers. This is intrinsically fulfilling.

Practice

» Breathe.
» Call to mind a work situation where your service was mediocre.
» Notice what is happening internally in your body and mind as you reflect on this.
» Now call to mind a time when you provided exceptional service in your work.
» Notice what is happening internally in your body and mind as you reflect this time.
» Notice the difference.
» Remind yourself that you can interrupt habitual patterns that do not serve you.

Fully engaged

As I arrived to the checkout counters, I searched for the shortest line. I noticed that six new automated self-help checkout machines had been installed but I still preferred the human touch. Waving, like a beacon of light, she signaled me to her counter. She made eye contact with me, smiled, and greeted me warmly. Fully engaged, she commented about the day, the weather, and newsworthy events. She did not rush me as I fumbled for my credit card to pay. She assisted with bagging my foodstuff rather than hovering and impatiently waiting for me to move on. She provided me with good service, and this had a positive and direct impact on my thoughts, my feelings, and my body.

Practice

> » Use all of your senses to be fully engaged in all who you interact with.
> » Make eye contact.
> » Go slowly, listen deeply.

Pizza boxes, landscapers, and a missed alarm clock

Twenty bags of soil were being delivered and placed at the back of the yard under the deck. The landscaper and I strolled to that location. Not only were the bags piled nicely, but a table was set, adorned with a table cloth, pizza, and six chairs. I turned in surprise, looked him in the eye with deep gratitude, and said, "Do you know what an impact you are making on people's lives?" I was grateful to have received good service in a dedicated and reliable fashion. Then I felt a hand on my shoulder and my Wise Wife woke me up.

You see, I had been dreaming about soil, pizza boxes, and landscapers, and missed hearing my alarm clock on this cold November morning. Yet there was a key message in that dream. We cannot underestimate the significance of our actions while at work. When we deliver in an admirable fashion, we help to ease the lives of others. Sometimes, years go by before we realize our impact. Mindfulness can assist us with this delivery. Wakeful, and no longer dreaming.

Practice

» Set your alarm clock to wake up 15 minutes earlier than usual.
» Go to a sitting mindfulness meditation posture.
» Anchor your awareness to the present moment with attention to the breath.
» Then reflect – How do I show up to those around me? What impact do I have on their life? Do I make a difference?

Light

Sometimes, I feel like a compassionate sleuth. I don't know if it is years of social work practice or a greater awareness and presence, or outcomes of my mindfulness practice, but I seem to have the ability to assess clients with a high level of accuracy. When I have these moments, I am acutely attuned, appropriately responsive, and deeply connected. I am able to understand meaning to stories that are tangential and outpouring. Together with the client, we are able to intertwine key themes that intersect theory and life. Clients often enter my office leery of how a social worker could possibly be of service and generally leave feeling empowered. Their context of viewing life's events often evolves from anxiety to exploration with openness, spaciousness, and curiosity. They see things more clearly and this gives them light. This is the essence of mindfulness.

Practice

» Be a compassionate sleuth today with full awareness and curiosity.
» Notice how this willingness to connect empowers.

The path eventually becomes comfortable

We were hit with a foot of snow, and as I shoveled to navigate out of the driveway, I had the following revelation. In many ways, we organize our patient's journey like we shovel snow. First, we assist them to slog through their mounds of pain and suffering, outlining a safe passageway while trying to not get stuck or bogged down in the process. Then, we begin our intervention gently and systematically, lifting layer after layer in an effort to expose what lies beneath. At times smooth pavement. Other times, rough terrain. Eventually, we work together to clear a pathway more defined and less insurmountable. The path eventually becomes comfortable and perhaps even well-trodden. This builds the foundation for the next snowfall and the one after that. The practice of mindfulness contributes to the development of this base. It helps us to see what is really there as we dig deep beneath the surface, and learn to trust that we can deal with whatever comes our way.

Practice

» Take some time to shovel beneath your layers.
» Breathe, pause, and dig deeper with curiosity and

non-judgment.
» Be gentle and kind.
» This is foundational in helping others.

A flower that blooms amongst the weeds

Just when we think that the healthcare system is laden with challenges, there can be a flower that blooms amongst the weeds. I crossed that line once again. The line that separates us from them. I became the patient. I was frightened and had no idea about how my journey would advance, but I was pleasantly surprised. In the midst of upheaval, I was treated kindly at hospital registration. My hand was held and staff looked into my eyes when they talked to me with sincerity. I was embraced by laboratory workers when I went for blood work. I was wished well by cleaning staff. Some staff told me that they would keep me in their thoughts. Others simply listened to my anguish. My physicians offered me hope and reinforced all would be okay. Nursing staff validated that my kind work with patients had been so appreciated and gave me permission to be a receiver of care, worthy. I am well today because they were all compassionate caregivers. They did not simply go through the motions. They offered me true presence every step of the way. Flowers in weeds.

Practice

» Sometimes our view of the flowers is obstructed by the weeds.
» Take time, today, to notice all that flourishes in spite of the obstacles.
» Allow for pleasant surprises to emerge.

The hug

Compassion comes in many forms. It comes with non-judgment. Not non-judgment in a rhetorical sense, but really opening up your heart and being present. Compassion comes from understanding your own vulnerability, so you too can understand the pain and suffering of others. Compassion comes from going the extra mile at the end of a tiring workday, when you just want to pack it all up and head home. Compassion grabs your heart and hangs on for dear life.

Today, while with a patient, I felt this reminder of being alive. A story was told. A plan was devised. Hope was restored. Then came the handshake and patient-requested hug. Do I back away? Do I gently tap her on the arm in a kind safe way or do I accept the hug? I chose the latter. It felt right and it was the compassionate thing to do.

Practice

» Take the time to honour the importance of touch.

A pediatric clinic pilgrimage

They arrived one by one like soldiers to our paediatric clinic to meet with the interdisciplinary team. I retrieved them and together we made our way to a large table to discuss the challenges of living with chronic illness. Some were bright eyed and respectful, eager to engage in sharing numbers and strategies, like sleuths trying to solve a mystery, while others sat with their heads downward, snarling with resentment. Some crafted long creative narratives of why and how they forgot to take care of their bodies while others simply shared that they just didn't care. Innuendos emerged. That unsaid, remained unsaid. It would have been so easy to judge, but instead, I chose to just listen.

Practice

» Listen first.
» Judge less.
» React from a place of wisdom and compassion.
» This is giving service.

Wisdom

The curtain closed and I laid on my stomach on the plinth. My physiotherapist went on to the next patient on the other side of the privacy curtain, adjacent to me. Machines and needles did their magic on this weathered body. I rested in the lull of the room and listened to conversations. One patient asked him where his son was, a young man training to follow his father's footsteps. He explained that his son was away as he was having his wisdom teeth removed. He joked that the lad had lost all of his wisdom. I chuckled while quietly listening. When we are mindful, we gain clarity and presence. We hear more acutely, feel more deeply, and act more wisely. This wisdom keeps us grounded so our actions are not knee-jerk but responsive.

Practice

» Breathe.
» Notice the wisdom of the mind and body.
» Don't lose it.

GRATITUDE

When we are in the thick of discomfort, we often only see negativity. We may feel sorry for ourselves. We cannot see the bigger picture as stress inhibits our ability to think straight. This contributes to tunnel vision and narrow thinking and this causes us to lose perspective. In our quest to survive, we become hijacked by fight, freeze or flee impulses. We become reactive rather than responsive. This is not entirely our fault as this is how we are physiologically wired. In the midst of this, we forget to acknowledge what we have to be grateful for. In order to feel grateful, we need to come into stillness long enough to reflect on what we have to be grateful for. We need to get off the hamster wheel that has taken away our ability to feel, to move beyond the default mode of negativity, cognizant of the bigger picture. When we are more mindful, we are able to do this. We begin to see the world in a different way, one where the glass is full rather than empty. The practice of mindfulness helps us to have more satisfying, kinder interactions with less impulsivity. This way of being cultivates gratitude.

A waltz of inquiry

I was sitting at my desk, trying to get through the day's demands, when one of the nurses came bolting into my office with a look of concern and a plea for help. This nurse felt uncertain about a patient and the potential risk of self-harm. I grabbed my pen and paper, and made my way to the nurse's office. There sat a frail soul hunched over on a seated walker, gaze looking down, in much physical and emotional discomfort. I connected to the patient immediately. Questions were skillful with purpose. The patient, although teary, was engaged, talkative, and with prodding, clear. Like a carpenter sculpting away at a piece of wood, the patient and I worked through a series of questions in a sequential manner, ruling out suicidal ideation. Our conversation became a dance. A tango of life or death. A waltz of inquiry.

Practice

- » Remind yourself that you are an expert craftsperson in all that you say and do.
- » Complete one task at a time, skillfully, with gratitude.

Smelly, germy, and busy

Smelly, germy, and busy – that is my description of an after-hours medical centre I find myself sitting in while waiting to see the doctor. I am surrounded by onlookers also waiting. I feel like they are watching my every move. They are coughing, huffing, fidgeting. I just want to go home, eat my dinner, and relax. I become present in the moment and find gratitude for my good health. Makes me compassionate and grateful.

Practice

> » Take a breath and arrive here, right now.
> » Call to mind a person or persons who make you feel uncomfortable.
> » Look for similarities rather than differences. We are all human. Look deeply.
> » Recognize that this person has had pain and suffering as you have.
> » Understand that everyone has a story to tell.
> » Open your heart to them.

Speechless

I was asked to do a presentation recently to one of our peer support programs. As I was leaving, a patient trailed my exit, clearly wanting to talk. He reminded me that we had seen one another a month prior. He explained that much had changed in his life. I stopped, looked at him in the eye, and reassured him of my presence. And in that moment, he looked back, grateful for my willingness to listen without interruption. He shared a terrible tragedy. He wept. He shared how grateful he was for the mindfulness practice that I had taught him and how it allowed him to get through this unexpected storm. I was speechless. I felt tremendous compassion and sadness for his loss. I felt honoured to have made a difference. I felt humbled by his inner strength and calm. I felt so grateful.

Practice

> » Breathe.
> » Call to mind a time when someone shared with you how you made a difference.
> » Notice what these words of gratitude elicit in thoughts, emotions, and body sensations.
> » Reflect on what you have learned.

I am free and my body belongs to me

It's 5:49 a.m. and I am sipping my coffee and simply being. Nowhere to go, nothing to do, no one to be. The hustle of city background noise has yet to arrive. It is mornings like these that invoke intense feelings of gratitude. I am fully aware that only two kilometres away sits a steel hospital fortress, a bastion of pain and suffering. I am grateful, today, for my health. I am free and my body belongs to me.

Practice

> » Be grateful for your body as it is in this moment.
> » Don't waste precious time with judgment.
> » Treat your body honourably.

We hear sadness so often that we forget to be open to gratitude

How does one measure outcome? Last week, a former patient phoned me. This patient had sustained a health setback and required further invasive treatment. They shared how they were practising mindfulness meditation prior to each treatment session and credited my past teachings for helping them to get through. The patient offered profound gratitude for making an immeasurable positive impact to their life. We so often sit with pain and suffering that we overlook all of the good that we bring. We hear sadness so often that we forget to be open to hearing gratitude.

Practice

» Be open to gratitude.
» Know that you truly make a difference.

Simply giving for the joy of doing so

I have a work colleague, Hilda, who loves to cook! She delights in her mindful preparation of feasts that she brings in to celebrate staff milestones or to simply surprise us. What inspires me the most about Hilda is her genuine ability to simply give for the joy of doing so. I have seen her with patients and her interactions are warm and caring. This makes a difference in their hospital visits. Yesterday, she celebrated my birthday and surprised me with a feast at lunch. We can learn so much from her generosity. I am so grateful to have Hilda as a mentor in this life lesson.

Practice

> » Give unselfishly for the joy of simply doing so with no
> expectations.

Dichotomy

Warm and muggy when it should be cool and crisp. Volatile and
antagonizing when she might have been kind and curious. Angry
and demonstrative when she could have been non-judgmental
and calm. A day full of dichotomy. As I walked home after work,
I approached a pathway that leads to a park signaling I am almost
home. This is usually a welcomed arrival, but today, it was even more
so. In the distance, I heard a woman on the other side of the fence
singing a melodic opera-like tune. I stopped and simply listened.
I felt grateful. Her voice was soothing and seemed to make all of
the day's contrasts make sense. Equanimity is a direct derivative of
mindfulness. It helps us to be with what is with uniform intensity
– in touch with reality but not seized by our emotions. When we
have equanimity in our life, we are able to delight in the music of
the moment.

Practice

> » Take a moment in your busyness to listen to a piece of
> music with full awareness.
> » Lying on your back, feet shoulder width apart, arms rest-
> ing on your sides with palms facing upwards.

» Listen with curiosity and freshness.
» Feel the flow, the rhythm, and the beats.
» Notice how it gradually increases with loudness, reaching a crescendo.
» Notice how it fades.
» See the contrasts.
» Follow the thread that ties it all together.
» This is equanimity.

A symphony

Our house was buzzing with much excitement and activity over dinner. Stories of the day were shared and laughter filled the room. Dinner was completed in increments, one by one, bit by bit. It all came together in symphony as each dinner guest arrived and departed. When the door closed and all had left, I sat and reflected content and quiet. Gatherings are comprised of unique persons with varied needs on individual paths. Be grateful for all contributions that gatherings elicit.

Practice

» A symphony is made up of four parts.
» Likewise, mindfulness has four foundations: body, breath, feelings, and teachings.
» When at a gathering, whether it be a celebration, a meal with friends and family, or a work meeting, take a moment to reflect on these four foundations of mindfulness that contribute to the symphony of awareness.
» Notice how the body is feeling.
» Notice the sensation of the breath.

» What feelings are emerging?
» What are the lessons to be learned?
» Be grateful and in harmony with all.

A wasteland

The wind howls, the house creaks, and crystallized snowflakes hit the windows, like a cascade of jagged bullets. The weatherman announces that the wind chill temperature has hit a grueling minus 38 degrees Celsius. Bones ache, my skin is a desert-like wasteland, and I dream of longer days with warmth and sunshine. The winter envelopes our existence and grips our pathways. With all that is barren and isolating, we are grateful for the shelter of our homes, the beauty of the everchanging sky, and the comforts that are unique to each of us.

Practice

» Come to stillness and notice what comforts you in barren times, such as fresh flowers, physical exercise, a warm cup of tea, a favourite sweater.
» Create the space to offer yourself comfort and self-compassion.

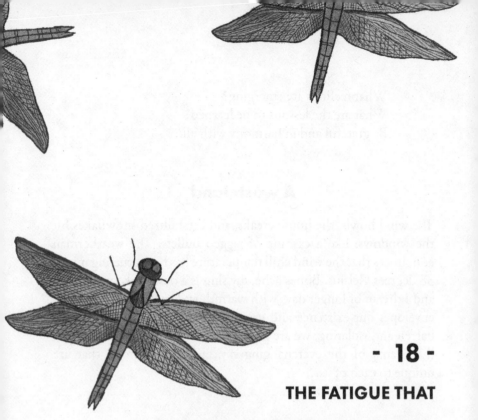

- 18 -

THE FATIGUE THAT

ACCOMPANIES CARING FOR OTHERS

When we are caregivers, we are often exposed to profound stories that leave an impermeable stain on us. This exposure can contribute to vicarious trauma, empathic distress, and burnout. Awareness derived through the practice of mindfulness helps us to recognize unhealthy patterns, behaviours, and the ways that we have adapted to this witnessed pain and suffering. This awareness is critical for self-care and change. Many of us have assumed caregiver roles. Some of us are simply born helpers. Our make-up is such that we are unequivocally touched by the suffering of others and we want to help. All of this caregiving requires that we reflect, refuel, and then reach out. Mindfulness can assist us with these three R's so that we can continue to care for others and stay afloat while doing so.

Buried

The winter has been unforgiving. We are buried in snow. Roofs are covered with blankets of immense white density. Roads are narrow, making passage difficult. Sidewalks are treacherous or nonexistent. Snow banks are so high that you can't see beyond them. Snow covering layers of ice, covering more snow. It all seems very heavy. In many ways, this is similar to the stress that we carry layer upon layer. We often just keep plugging along, masters at distraction and busyness. But over time, our thinking becomes narrow and our clarity obstructed. This way of coping becomes overtaxing and takes a toll on our wellbeing. We become judgmental. This is why it is so important for us to take time to go to silence for replenishment. Mindfulness helps us to break free from heaviness and to know that spring is on the horizon.

Practice

> » The time in between work and home can be a wonderful opportunity to pause.
> » Find a quiet space away from distraction and busyness.
> » Allow for mindful reflection and insight.
> » Be open to what is unearthed.

They remember

The patient seemed unfriendly and detached on the telephone. As our conversation progressed, he elaborated about negative experiences with previous healthcare providers. He was clear to state that in his opinion healthcare providers were equivalent to mechanics. He explained further that he should be able to direct them on what to work on and the rest was none of their concern. I tried to heighten his awareness to the importance of whole person care but he did not wish to hear about it. Body and mind are inseparable. You cannot take care of one and neglect the other. Mindfulness is a link between both. Mindfulness helps us to understand the mechanics of being right here, right now, paying attention to what is happening in our heart, mind, and body.

Practice

» Remember that body and mind are inseparable.
» The body and mind both remember.

Not tonight, honey

"Let's do something fun and off the cuff tonight," I suggested to my Wise Wife following the adrenaline rush of a run. The morning was sunny and the harshness of the winter seemed to be behind us. Full of energy, I walked to work, and immersed myself into another busy day. After dinner that evening, my wife gently reminded me of my morning intention. She suggested going to the cinema at 6:30 p.m. My response was, "not tonight, honey, it's too late."

Although I had ambitious intentions at the beginning of my day, by day's end my quest for adventure quickly dwindled as did my energy. We never know how our days will unravel. This is where the importance of self-compassion and non-judgment become relevant.

Practice

» Our bodies, energy levels, and daily demands all fluctuate.
» It takes awareness, openness, and wisdom to listen to what they are telling us.
» Drop judgment.

Preoccupied

There is a fine line between being supportive and needing to be firm. He sat in front of me. His eyes squinted and appeared vacant... disassociated. I judged. Was he on drugs? How could he not even be able to tell me his age? Does he even care? His every answer seemed mechanical. He simply uttered repetitively "fine...fine... fine." Was I working much harder than he was? Why did I even care if he didn't seem to? My agenda said I was present. The sign on my door told others I was occupied but perhaps preoccupied was more the case. I will try again, but this time with an open and curious mind.

Practice

» When with a friend, family member or work colleague, notice.
» Where are you?
» Are you distracted?
» Trust that you will have the required resources to deal with all of what you are thinking about later.
» Now come back to the present moment with gratitude and mindful presence.

Her downward spiral

If I had a health problem, she is the healthcare professional that I would want. She is genuine, cares, and is passionate about her work. She understands illness. She would be direct but gentle with my provision of care. This saddens me because she has become emotionally impulsive and is exhibiting signs of burnout. She blames, is cynical, and her body language tells a story of fatigue and exhaustion. Her behaviours are governed by explosiveness and rigidity. She has managed to isolate herself from her co-workers, which adds to her downward spiral. She needs help but no one knows how to tell her. She is not ready to look in the mindfulness mirror and to sit with what is. I hope she is ready soon.

Practice

> »　Arrive to the here and now with the breath.
> »　Are you able to recognize any of these signs of fatigue and exhaustion in caring for others?
> »　Dig deeper.
> »　Are you ready to make change?

Do you ever just reach the point of saturation?

My last patient of the day clung hold of me like a child clings to their parent's leg. Every time I attempted to bring the interview to a close, she rambled on. I wanted to be compassionate as a human being, but I was also aware that I wanted to move away to a remote cabin in the woods and be left alone. I fulfilled all roles professionally. When the interview finally concluded, I found myself scrambling in haste to pack my bag, retreating to the parking lot as fast as I could and driving feverishly to just get home. I immediately went to the cushion to meditate and felt more grounded.

Practice

> » Do something completely for you today.
> » This is not selfish.
> » It is required.

Unstuck

My eldest daughter, Blue Eyes, wears a ring we gave her on her twenty first birthday. But for some reason, her finger was swollen and the ring could not be removed. All efforts to get it off resulted in more frustration, screams, and further swelling. We attempted to remove it with ice, soap, and baby oil with no success. We were ready to simply go to the local ER and get it removed (the ring, not the finger!) but the six-foot, four-inch giant living with us for the summer had another idea. He is an electrician by trade, as clever as a whip, and loves to solve puzzles. He was bound and determined to solve this riddle. Systematically, he used dental floss, wrapped it around the finger and tugged. Millimeter by millimeter the ring moved gently upwards and off.

At times, we too feel saturated and stuck in the roles that we play, the places that we work in and the families that we are part of. This subtle undercurrent is limiting and eventually takes a toll on our happiness. Hope, self-compassion, and mindfulness helps us to get unstuck.

Practice

- » Take ten minutes to come to stillness.
- » Consider a situation that repeats itself and your way of handling it.
- » With conscious awareness be open to other ways of responding to this situation.
- » Observe what comes up by being open to a different way.

Safe harbour

Conversation fills the room – the guy who lost his limb, the woman who has unforgiving illness, the young boy who resists taking his medication, the angry man who left abruptly. Sometimes, these stories in the lunchroom are just too much. The place that is supposed to be a safe harbour that will nourish us both physically and emotionally, becomes a place of judgment. In my work, we are present with much suffering. Disgust becomes laughter. Laughter feeds a questioning of moral ethics. Guilt emerges, if only for a minute. The lunchroom conversation continues.

Practice

- » Find a place where you are able to eat alone in silence.
- » This can be a powerful healer.

The trenches

"Let the battle rounds begin," echoed words from the television as the singing competition show commenced last evening. Then, one of the judges talked about "flawless execution" and "passion" demonstrated in a contestant's performance. This made me think about the daily challenges I face in the trenches of frontline healthcare work. The people that I interact with may be scared and this fear can get projected to me as they grumble, speak sharply, and respond with one-word replies. Their pain vicariously becomes my pain. We may try to distance ourselves but our souls remain connected. Our execution becomes flawed. Our passion gets derailed.

Practice

- » Breathe.
- » Bring to mind a recent unpleasant conversation.
- » What did this bring out in you?
- » Were you reactive or responsive?
- » Had you taken a moment to pause, breathe, and check in physically, emotionally, and cognitively might you have responded in a different way?
- » How can you apply this the next time that you encounter this situation?

Why had I waited so long?

Why is it that we are so easily apt to take care of others but forget the requirement of taking care of self? While in Dublin, Ireland recently, I came across an old-fashioned barber shop with a sign outside advertising fresh shaves. I commented on it and quickly went on my way. As the day went by, I began to think about practicing what I preach with self-care. I later returned to the barbershop and was warmly greeted by a young man who confirmed that I was there for a shave. This whole concept seemed self-indulgent and foreign to me. I fondly reminisced about frequenting a barber shop with my father as a boy and squirmed with the idea of someone putting a straight razor to my neck presently. First, I experienced the joy of having a hot towel cradled around my face. This was to soften. Then, came the shaving cream lathered in a repetitive circular motion over and over again. I melted into the chair. Then, appeared a razor. By this time, my apprehension had dissipated. I relaxed in this experience and asked myself why had I waited so long?

Practice

» Think about an item on your selfcare wish list that you have been putting off.
» Perhaps something that you view as unnecessary and undeserving.
» Now, pause, notice where you are feeling the effects of this procrastination in your body.
» Now go ahead and indulge.

A strong façade

My youngest daughter, Brown Eyes, travelled home to surprise my Wise Wife, who was celebrating her launch into retirement. Her arrival stirred up many emotions. The climactic goodbye at the airport two months ago seemed distant. I had a calmer acceptance that we could do this. I justified that the flight was doable and the 3000 kilometer distance, manageable. I felt less overwhelmed about her move to Alberta, more self-assured.

At the end of the weekend, we said new goodbyes at the airport and waved through the plexiglass as we walked to the parked car. A huge surge of emotion swept my inner being. I sat there and wept. I missed my Brown Eyes. Her departure was not as easy as I had anticipated that it would be. It tugged at my heart, and resonated with me for days.

Although we may plan to be strong in our work, our hearts are often pulled by raw emotion. On the surface, we may portray a strong facade, but the pain that we experience as compassionate caregivers churns a quieter hidden suffering.

Practice

» Bring attention to a situation that raises emotion.
» Sit with the emotion and allow it to be felt.
» Trust your ability to be with it.

Drowning

My colleague is working himself to death. His day is comprised of 90% work and 10% for other living tasks. His friends include headaches, depression, fatigue, and insomnia. His body has become a host to re-current infections. He is in constant high alert. He feels like he is drowning and he will not recognize maladaptive coping patterns that he has mindlessly adapted to stay afloat. He ignores health issues. He does not feel that he can afford to get sick. No matter how much we try to strategize small tangible goals to help mitigate his work stress and divert this imbalance, he finds reasons why he is unable to make change. He will sink and we will have to compassionately swim to his rescue. He has something valuable to teach us today. Our body eventually says no.

Practice

- » Take a moment to breathe.
- » Check in.
- » Listen.
- » Learn.

Dad, listen to this...

"Do you think it could be birds nesting in the bathroom exhaust fan?" asked Brown Eyes over the telephone. The chirping sounds confirmed it – most definitely birds. The weather has been unseasonably cold in Edmonton, so one could easily understand the birds' instinct to find shelter to stay warm. Our world feels unseasonably cold right now. There is judgment, unkindness, and divisiveness. Many are suffering. The birds nesting are not unlike human beings, who want to stay in bed and pull the covers up a little higher. The birds will be evicted today. We need to be with what is.

Practice

- » Recognize how you react with cumulative stress.
- » Do you try to shelter yourself from it?
- » Where does it show up in your body?
- » Are you able to sit with it?

Don't look back

The sound of silence begins to emerge. Office lights out, one by one. A couple of farewells uttered. Some chatter in the distance. The crescendo of busyness has begun to retreat. The endless flow of workplace demands has entered the ebb phase. Pack up those Christmas treats, lock up your file drawers and lay down the "to-do" lists. It's time to rest and enter a new flow phase necessary for renewal. Don't look back as the door shuts and don't look forward to the lists of things posted on your message board. Take some time to simply be in the moment, mindfully.

Practice

- »   Periodically throughout your day, pause. Stop and notice.
- »   Remind yourself...when you are at work, you are at work.
- »   Remind yourself...when you are at home, you are at home.
- »   Don't look forward.
- »   Don't look back.
- »   Just be.

Self-contained communities of hope, compassion, and mutual respect

Last night, I had the opportunity to attend a photo exhibit at the library, presented by a friend, who had recently travelled to India. Each photo that he shared in his presentation told an important story. Images included: city laundrymen, who painstakingly cleaned laundry in hundreds of stalls and then hung it outside on miles of clotheslines; to the tea harvesters, who picked three leaves at a time infinitely. Communities appeared proud and self-sustaining, and no job was viewed as inferior or unimportant. There were no egos, just a sense of working together to survive. Imagine if we could adopt this philosophy in the places that we live and work. Imagine an eradication of divisive rules, replaced by visions that build. Imagine self-contained mindful communities of hope, compassion, and mutual respect.

Practice

» If you were to take a photograph of your work setting, family, or neighbourhood what would you see?
» How would these images resonate with you in mind, body and emotion?
» Are you able to see clearly with beginners eyes?
» What would you change, if anything?
» Can you commit to going forward, and incorporating some of the mindfulness practices that you have learned towards the creation of a more mindful community?
» What concrete ways can you do this?

Epilogue

Every so often it takes a life event or happening to cause you to pause and reflect. The machine becomes self-propelled, tireless, sometimes without you even being aware of it, even when you are on a personal mindfulness journey of becoming more aware. In many ways, these midweek mindfulness personal stories and insights have followed a similar path. The target audience that I wrote for has changed since its inception, but my hope is that it continues to find presence in the hearts of those who have moved on. Many of the list serve members are new, and do not know the roots of this sangha. How does that differ from the rest of us who wake up each day, go to work, be with our families and go to sleep? In autopilot we forget where we have come from, what is important and not so important to us in our lives until something or someone comes along to remind us. Perhaps the lesson is that we trust that things will unfold in their own accord. Perhaps we need to stop long enough to observe and have the patience to look deeper.

The person who reached out in a time of need emailed the group the next day. Six months prior she had applied for a job, been granted an interview and not heard back, that is until the day following our first midweek mindfulness meditation that sent her loving kindness from around the globe. She shared that she was offered a new job and asked to start the next day. She thanked the group profusely for their messages of encouragement, employment offers, and sharing of their own life struggles. She attributed her good fortune to the power of connection and the group. She defined this experience as miraculous, but I like to think of it as simply doing what we needed to do in that moment. She suggested that the midweek mindfulness meditation continue so that others could benefit in some way from its presence.

Change is inevitable. When the first midweek mindfulness meditation was shared, I had just embarked on completing my Masters of Social Work degree. This immersion into a world of academia, satisfied my thirst for knowledge and revived passion to make a difference. I left generalized medical social work practice and specialized to working with persons with kidney disease where suffering was robust. Years elapsed and I soon found myself working in the world of diabetes care, helping many to be with this chronic illness. Through the years, my mindfulness practice also developed parallel to my professional and personal lives.

I am now credentialed to teach Mindfulness-Based Stress Reduction through the Center for Mindfulness in Medicine, Health Care, and Society at the University of Massachusetts Medical School. I continue to run but I am no longer able to complete marathons, although I secretly dream of running just one more. My hair is a bit thinner, my step a bit quieter, my body achier, and my tendency to be pulled into life's drama less likely.

My Wise Wife continues to be the strong woman that she has always been, but a little gentler to herself along the path, and even wiser. She co-teaches Mindfulness-Based Stress Reduction with me and together we have had the joy of bringing this life changing curriculum to community. I am honoured to learn from her and share my passion of mindfulness with her. She too is qualified to teach Mindfulness-Based Stress Reduction (MBSR) through the Center for Mindfulness in Medicine, Health Care, and Society at the University of Massachusetts Medical School. Together we have co-created Mindfulness on the Rocks: Meditation Solutions for Maximum Life Impact with a goal of creating a more mindful society.

Brown Eyes has emerged from being a teenager to a gifted teacher who works in the elementary school system, gently guiding the children who are so fortunate to learn from her. She has completed the Mindfulness-Based Stress Reduction program and adapted mindfulness practices in her classroom knowing the value of this for her students. She is now married to the Giant Sandwich Maker, now an electrical apprentice who has also completed the Mindfulness-Based Stress Reduction program. Little does he know that he has been our teacher, helping us to understand the importance of stopping and looking with infectious curiosity and open eyes.

Blue Eyes has transitioned from a high school student to a physiotherapist in a hospital setting mindful of the body's strengths and limitations, guiding patients to honour their bodies with gentleness and kindness. She and her husband, The Hunch, hike each weekend in nature, respectful of what they need, to reconnect and to slow down in this busy world. He is a caring optometrist who recognizes the importance of seeing through a new lens and the value of beginners eyes. Both have also completed the Mindfulness-Based Stress Reduction program. Both give with much kindness. They have blessed me with a first grandchild that I cannot get enough of each day. This new life will teach all of us more about mindfulness than we could ever imagine. For this I am so grateful.

And so, my parting words can be summarized in the following. Live life to the fullest, learn from all that it throws your way, have fun in your work and your daily living, love deeply, stop to look into the eyes of your children, be with others who are suffering with true presence, and know that you make a difference. Lastly, take a chance and Respond, with full mindfulness awareness.

Acknowledgments

I would like to thank Sheila, the love of my life for her ongoing support and mentorship. As an MBSR teacher Sheila understands the ethos of mindfulness, embodies it, and keeps me true to the teachings. She inspires me daily and nurtures my passion in this work.

I am grateful to our two beautiful daughters, Emily and Hannah, for their ongoing support and for allowing me to be fully present with them through life. I also appreciate the love and support from Jason and Scott, our two new family members.

I am grateful to Latitude 46 Publishing, Laura and Heather, for their interest, professional guidance, and ongoing support in helping to make this book a reality from my home community of Sudbury, Ontario.

I would like to thank The National Kidney Foundation, USA and the Council of Nephrology Social Workers for their leadership's and membership's encouragement and support in developing the Midweek Meditation, always encouraging my professional contribution to the organization and to the entire Chronic Kidney Disease circle of care.

And lastly, I am grateful to the very special person who reached out by email to the list server group in June 2011. I am grateful to have met her through her message. I had the privilege to respond and it is the response that sparked this undertaking. She is the impetus behind this endeavour.

Keep in touch with Gary

Website: www.mindfulnessontherocks.ca

Email: hello@mindfulnessontherocks.ca